St Matthew's Gospel

A COMMENTARY

NORMAN PRICE

RELIGIOUS AND MORAL EDUCATION PRESS
An Imprint of Pergamon Press

Religious and Moral Education Press
Hennock Road, Exeter EX2 8RP
An Imprint of Pergamon Press

Pergamon Press Ltd
Headington Hill Hall, Oxford OX3 0BW

Pergamon Press Inc.
Maxwell House, Fairview Park, Elmsford, New York 10523

Pergamon Press Canada Ltd
Suite 104, 150 Consumers Road, Willowdale, Ontario M2J 1P9

Pergamon Press (Australia) Pty Ltd
P.O. Box 544, Potts Point, N.S.W. 2011

Pergamon Press GmbH
Hammerweg 6, D–6242 Kronberg, Federal Republic of Germany

First published 1985

Printed in Great Britain by A. Wheaton & Co. Ltd, Exeter

ISBN 0 08-031786-3 non net
ISBN 0 08-031787-1 net

Contents

Acknowledgements

The author and publisher wish to thank the following for permission to reproduce photographs in this book.

Associated Press: p.15
Britain/Israel Public Affairs Committee: pp.17, 22, 25, 35, 53, 69, 71, 80, 90, 95, 103, 113 (Richard Nowitz, W2PS)
The Mansell Collection: p.12

The cover photograph is taken from the Book of Cerne and is reproduced by permission of the Syndics of Cambridge University Library.

Introduction

The study of the Christian religion is a challenging and exciting subject, not least in the sense that new ideas and information are continually coming to light and need to be explored and analysed, especially regarding Biblical material and the understanding of the Christian faith. It has always been my belief and experience that from sound and sensible study of such material many other issues and considerations – moral, ethical, social and even political – could and should arise. The Bible should not be treated as a museum piece, or as a hot-house plant to be protected from every cold wind of criticism; if it is to be seen as relevant today, it must undergo the same scrutiny with regard to its value and truths as do other areas of study.

With this in mind, I have produced some commentaries on the gospels. My notes are a gathering together of research, ideas, questions and discussions over many years of preparing candidates for examinations in Religious Studies, though they are not intended only for the class-room but for all would-be students of the gospels, of all ages, denominations and backgrounds.

The first commentary was on Mark, because that was the first gospel to appear. The next one was on Luke, showing how he used some of Mark's material and added to it from his own sources. Now we have Matthew and we can see how the author uses most of Mark's material, together with his own special material, as well as drawing on a source common to both Matthew and Luke. With this third commentary the 'synoptic' pattern is seen more clearly and some of its problems clarified.

Teachers and students alike will be aware that examiners are always looking for evidence from candidates of up-to-date background information, together with the candidates' own assessment and evaluation of ideas, incidents and characters. I have therefore incorporated these requirements into the notes. I have not included a text of the gospel because I have always found it a rewarding exercise to consult as many different translations as possible, provided that they are read in conjunction with the notes. For that purpose, full chapter and verse references are given throughout.

I have worked within a definite framework of requirements for G.C.E. O level and similar examinations and it is obvious that, in this kind of commentary, every aspect and incident cannot be dealt with at great length. However, there are plenty of suggestions and ideas which I hope will be explored and developed by the student as time and opportunity allow.

Norman Price
Head of Religious Studies
Torquay Grammar School

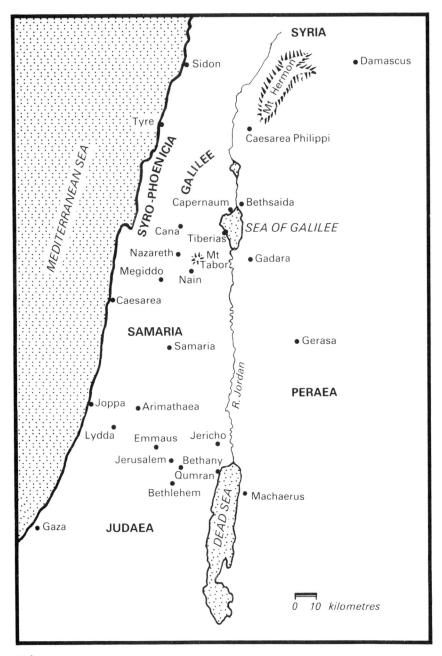

Palestine

Matthew, the Author

The order of the gospels

Most people can recite the canon or order of the gospels in the New Testament as Matthew, Mark, Luke and John, but many are surprised to learn that although that was the sequence in which they were placed by the early Church it was almost certainly not the order in which they were written or, at least, in which they first appeared.

The question of why they were placed in that order is of interest not only to modern scholars, but has been the subject of controversy ever since the second century. As far as we can tell, it was about the middle of that century that the 'gospel', which was the 'good news' brought and taught by Jesus and first passed on in oral form by eyewitnesses, began to take on its now familiar 'fourfold' appearance and the written records became known as 'According to Matthew', 'According to Mark', and so on.

From those very early days these have been the only four to be recognized as authentic. There were other accounts of the life of Jesus, but these were not accepted as genuine, although some were supposed to have been written by disciples, e.g. 'The Gospel of Thomas'. These have now become known as the apocryphal (hidden) gospels.

Why was Matthew placed first?

All four gospels were in use by the middle of the second century and Christian writers quoted from them all. However, Matthew emerged as the favourite, as far as quotations were concerned, and Ignatius, Bishop of Antioch in Syria in about A.D. 115, showed particular preference for it. So it was really a matter of popularity rather than order of publication. Today, although many people maintain that they prefer the beauty of Luke's account or the majesty of John's gospel, in terms of church services and liturgy Matthew is still the most widely used. Denominations as diverse as the Roman Catholic Church and Christian Scientists appeal to it as the main support for their doctrines.

It was almost certainly the first gospel to be accepted by a great centre of the Christian faith, probably Antioch in Syria, although some scholars suggest the centre was Aleppo or Edessa. It soon took preference over Mark's gospel, which was already being read in Rome, mainly because it was more complete than Mark's and seemed to clarify many of the issues which Mark had left 'in the air'.

The gospel according to Luke took a little longer to be accepted, probably because it was said to be connected with a man named Marcion, who had a

1

reputation as a heretic! Finally, the gospel according to John was given fourth place because although it didn't fit in very well with the other three it was obviously of tremendous spiritual value in interpreting the life of Jesus. So, after many years and much discussion, the canon took its present form, though there was apparently never any doubt as to Matthew having first place.

Was the author Matthew the disciple?

There is no clear answer to this. In the equating of the four living creatures from the Book of Revelation (4: 6–8) with the four gospel writers, Matthew is represented by the man, presumably because of his desire to portray Jesus as the Jewish Messiah, a descendant of David. However, this does not help much in identifying 'Matthew' the man and the author.

Most scholars maintain that the gospel writer was not the disciple. The main reasons for this are as follows.

1. The fact that a gospel was given the title 'According to...' is not proof that a particular person wrote it.
2. This gospel does not give the impression of being the work of an eyewitness, although it is the kind of methodical approach which fits in well with the way a tax-collector's mind may have worked. Surely, it is argued, a disciple would have given much more indication of his personal involvement? Although, to balance this, it could be said that Matthew was never a prominent member of the Twelve.
3. The writer relies very heavily on Mark's gospel. He takes some 600 verses from Mark's 660, then reduces them to about 500 of his 1068 verses. To do that, he edits, rearranges, rewrites and, some would say, even corrects Mark's material, in addition to tidying up Mark's often careless Greek grammar. It is obvious that Matthew had a copy of Mark's writing from which he worked. It seems unlikely that one of the disciples would have described in another man's words, events that he himself witnessed, especially since the other writer was not one of the Twelve and his work was regarded, for a time at least, as of secondary importance.
4. Mark writes very plainly of what seem to be frequent failures by the disciples to understand what Jesus meant or even, at times, to be much help to Jesus at all! Matthew is dismayed by such frankness and in his copying either moderates the references or omits them altogether. It seems logical that a disciple would have hesitated to excuse himself and his fellow disciples in this way, but a later writer may have wanted to safeguard their reputations.

To balance these suggestions other evidence must also be taken into account. A fragment of a document written by Papias, Bishop of Hierapolis in Syria in about A.D. 140 – and quoted by the historian Eusebius in about

2

A.D. 325 – says, 'Matthew made an orderly compilation of the logia of the Lord in the Hebrew language and each one translated them as he was able'. That, at first sight, seems to indicate that Matthew the disciple was the author. However, the gospel of Matthew is a Greek gospel, not a translation from the Hebrew (or Aramaic, as Papias probably meant) and there is no evidence of a Hebrew original. Moreover, Papias wrote of the 'logia' or sayings of Jesus, not of a 'gospel', and it is known that there *was* a collection in written form of the sayings of Jesus. This collection was used by both Matthew and Luke. The document (which is no longer in existence) has become known as 'Q' from the German word 'Quelle' meaning 'Source'.

This document was almost certainly written in Aramaic and was translated and used by various writers as they wanted it. Many think that Matthew was the author of 'Q', in which case he was a contributor to this gospel, since it uses quite a lot of 'Q'; even so, this does not prove that 'Matthew' was the disciple. What *is* regarded by many as a clue to the writer's identity occurs in Chapter 13, Verse 52, which mentions a 'teacher of the Law' – probably a scribe – becoming 'a disciple'. He was apparently a Greek-speaking Jew who had become a Christian and a 'convert to the Kingdom'.

The main aims of Matthew's gospel

During recent years much research has been done on how, why, when and where the gospels were written. Some of the results have helped to reduce the mystery surrounding the gospels, while others have raised further problems. One thing seems clear: each gospel writer used his material to suit his own particular purpose. Mark wrote for persecuted Christians who badly needed encouragement; Luke had the 'outsiders' very much in mind; Matthew's account was meant for Jewish Christians in the early Church.

Like Mark, Matthew wrote at a time of crisis, but of a different kind. He wrote at a time when the Church was expanding rapidly and missionaries were taking the gospel to many places. There was an urgency to 'proclaim the good news' but also to safeguard the gospel against heretics and enemies. That is why Matthew puts great emphasis on the need for authority and on Christian leadership. There were all kinds of attacks on the Church and Matthew's 'missionary manual', as it has been called, was designed to refute these.

Moreover, he was writing to Jewish readers who had many questions in their minds about the new Movement, such as: was the Messiah a descendant of David? Did he interpret the Laws and traditions of Moses? Was his life and ministry a fulfilment of Old Testament prophecies? To all these questions, Matthew answers, 'Yes'. He puts great store on the way the Old Testament was fulfilled; he uses about a hundred direct and indirect examples. In fact, at times he is so anxious to do this that he tries either to

3

shape the Scriptures to fit the facts or, it seems, to make the facts fit the Scriptures!

Matthew portrays Jesus as the giver of the New Law, not only by likening him to Moses going up the mountain (Chapters 5,6 and 7), but also by the way in which the gospel is arranged in five teaching sections, which are meant to represent the Pentateuch, the first five books of the Bible (this is the Jewish Torah, often referred to by Christians as 'The Five books of Moses'). These sections, as we shall see, form the teaching nucleus of various themes. They are:

1. The new teaching of Jesus on the Law (Chs 5–7)
2. Instructions to the disciples (Ch. 10)
3. Parables about the Kingdom (Ch. 13)
4. Problems in the Church (Ch. 18)
5. Teaching on Judgement and the Kingdom (Chs 24–25)

This is the only gospel to use the world 'Church' (16: 18, 18: 17), and the way in which the writer does so suggests that he saw the Church as much more of an organization than the original Aramaic word of Jesus would have meant. It is also a gospel of 'the King and the Kingdom', with many of the parables beginning 'The Kingdom of heaven is like...'. The writer obviously believed, or at least hoped, that the Kingdom would come in the near future. So it is not surprising that this gospel fitted in well with the life of the early Church. It looked not only back to the traditions of the past, but forward to the future with great hope and expectation.

Sources of Information

As well as using most of Mark's gospel, Matthew includes some of the 'Q' material which is also found in Luke's gospel, though at times Matthew seems to use it in a different way. The scholar G.H. Streeter has referred to the material found only in Matthew as the 'M' source, whilst Bacon has suggested that there was a further source which he called the 'Narazene' or 'N' source. The thing to bear in mind, I believe, is that Matthew didn't merely borrow from Mark or anyone else, but, having deliberately selected the material he wanted, used it to build his own structure, following Mark's plan but adding his own 'extensions' and sometimes 'supports', until he had created the kind of construction he wanted.

Date

When this gospel appeared is not easy to say with much accuracy and scholars are by no means unanimous in their opinions. Some give it an early date, even saying that it was the first gospel to be written. However, most are agreed that it was written some time after the fall of Jerusalem, in

A.D. 70, but before A.D. 96 because Clement, Bishop of Rome at that time, evidently knew of it. Therefore they give it a date of about A.D. 85.

As a 'life of Christ' Matthew's gospel is regarded by many as the least valuable, but as a 'treasure-house' of Jesus's teaching it is very highly prized. Perhaps that is why the nineteenth-century French writer Renan, having described Luke's gospel as 'the most beautiful book in the world', went on to call Matthew's gospel 'the most important book in the world'.

The Text

CHAPTER 1   THE BEGINNINGS

All four gospels begin with a brief prologue in which the writer states his main aims and purpose in writing and in which the reader can see some of the themes that are to be developed later on.

Mark begins with the blunt statement that it is 'the gospel of Jesus Christ, the son of God'. It is 'good news' – this is the meaning of the Anglo-Saxon 'God-spel' and the Greek 'evangelion' – but it was brought by a Messiah who was a suffering servant. Luke says that he has decided to write a 'connected narrative' in order to pass on 'authentic knowledge', having 'gone over the whole course of these events in detail'. John starts in a different way, using symbolism to explain *why* Jesus was born.

Matthew begins with a family tree in which he traces Jesus's ancestry back to King David to show that Jesus was the true Messiah and had royal authority by direct descent.

vv. 1–17   The roots

Such genealogies, to give this family tree its proper name, were not uncommon in Jewish families and were used, for example, to establish a priestly descent. Since they were usually accurate for only a few generations, this one going back about eighteen hundred years would have been very unusual! Matthew follows the traditional Jewish pattern of putting such a statement of origin at the beginning. Luke (3: 23–38) prefers to put it later, when Jesus begins his work. Perhaps Matthew had in mind the words of Genesis 5: 1, 'This is the record of the descendants of Adam'.

The reasons   The first verse is like the language of an official document because to the writer the list has the authority of Scripture to show the sovereignty of Jesus, descendant of David, the King of Israel. But we would be mistaken to think of it as a legal document, dealing only with descendants in the strictly physical sense. Matthew's main aim in this first chapter is to combine the royal descent with the miraculous birth. It was a combination of the physical and the spiritual, of history and miracle. Jesus was the Messiah both by birth and by the will of God.

The revelation   The purpose of the ancient 'tables of ancestry' was not always to show an accurate descent but rather to demonstrate the importance of a particular person. In this case the writer is presenting Jesus as the 'Christ', the 'anointed one'. This comes from the Greek word

'Christos'; the Hebrew 'Mashiah', from which we get 'Messiah', means the same. It was a term often applied to one who was anointed with holy oil, such as a high priest (Leviticus 4: 3) or a king (1 Samuel 10: 1). So 'Christ' was not a name, it was a title. He was Jesus *the* Christ. 'Jesus' is the Latin form of the Greek 'Iesous'. The Hebrew was 'Jehoshua' or Joshua, so as a boy Jesus would have been known in Nazareth as Joshua-bar-Joseph ('bar' = son of).

The record (vv. 2–16, Luke 3: 23–38)   In the three groups that he gives Matthew seems to be more interested in the symbolism of the 'tree' than in the accuracy of its 'branches'. It is surprising that such an expert on Jewish history did not check his list more carefully. For example, only the first group corresponds to the actual generations recorded in the Old Testament. (What is known to Christians as the 'Old Testament' is the complete Jewish Bible.) Most of the names in the third group are almost impossible to identify, whilst the second group has some strange gaps between generations. Another point to note is the inclusion of women's names. There are four, of whom only Ruth is not associated in some way with immorality.

Why are there three groups?   (By contrast, Luke's list contains seventy-six names.) All sorts of suggestions have been made, ranging from the possibility that it was purely accidental to the idea that the three represented the rise, decline and restoration of the Hebrew kingdom. Certainly, three was seen as a *complete* number, having a beginning, middle and end. As we shall see in this gospel, Matthew seems to have a special affection for the number seven, and fourteen is twice seven! In fact, his claim (v. 17) that there were three groups of fourteen generations is not quite accurate: in the third group, including Jesus, there are only thirteen.

One of the more intriguing possibilities is that since the consonants in the Hebrew word 'David' add up to the value of fourteen (i.e. the fourth, the sixth and the fourth letter), the lists are symbolic for that sovereign. However, the real reason may be much simpler. Mention of Solomon's mother, Bathsheba, would remind Matthew's readers of an ugly incident in David's life (2 Samuel 11), so perhaps this genealogy was a reminder that even men regarded as 'great' were in need of the blessing which the birth of the Messiah would bring.

What is the point of tracing Jesus's ancestry back through Joseph if it were a virgin birth?   The birth stories, both in Matthew and in Luke, bristle with difficulties of which this is one. Another question is why Mary needed to marry at all if the child were not Joseph's. The point is that through Joseph, as Mary's husband though not Jesus's father, in the physical sense, the right to David's throne would be transferred to Mary's child. In addition, Mary would be protected by the love and respectability of a husband. Even in the gospels we see some insulting remarks about Jesus's origin, e.g. John 8: 48, where his Jewish birth and background are questioned.

vv. 18–25   The realization
Matthew makes no bones about the birth of Jesus. He paints the picture with bold strokes.

Mary was promised to Joseph in marriage and in Jewish law such a betrothal was binding, so much so that if her fiancé died, the promised girl was then considered a widow. Such an agreement could not be broken off merely by mutual consent of both parties; the man had to give the girl a 'writ of divorce' or note of dismissal for the espousal, as it is often called, to be ended (Deuteronomy 24: 1). That is why the translation 'Do not fear to take Mary, your wife, into your home' (v.20) is correct. She *was* regarded as Joseph's wife, but the marriage was not formally recognized until the wedding took place and the bridegroom took the bride to his home. But before all that happened Mary found she was going to have a baby 'by the Holy Spirit'.

The dilemma (v.19)   Joseph's name came from the Hebrew 'yasaph', meaning 'may God add', but it also contained the sound of the verb 'asaph', 'he takes away'. In Genesis 30: 23–24, the writer cleverly uses both meanings for Jacob's son, but here Joseph must have wondered which meaning applied, for first Mary had been given to him and now it seemed she was being taken away.

But Joseph was a 'just man' or 'righteous man' or 'man of principle'; the words vary according to which translation is used, but the meaning is the same. He wanted to do the right thing, but what was that? He loved Mary and wanted her as his wife, but he also wanted to keep within the law. So he could either ask a court to hear the case, which would mean a public hearing and accusations, or he could save her from that disgrace by giving her a private letter of divorce, in the presence of two witnesses, which would mean there was no need to make it public.

Does that mean that he thought she was guilty of wrong-doing?   Not necessarily. In fact, it seems to show that he wanted to give her the benefit of the doubt. He was no doubt upset and bewildered by it all, but he was more concerned about Mary than he was about himself. The Greek word Matthew uses for 'just' implies not only religious scruple but also sensitivity and kindness. He had decided to treat Mary in the best possible way he could *before* he knew the truth, which is a great testimony to his trust.

The dream (v.20)   Matthew uses the traditional Biblical example of a dream to show how Joseph's problem was resolved. The Greek word translated as 'dream' meant 'instructed by God', but in classical Greek the word had a commercial sense and meant 'to do business'. Matthew, unlike Luke, does not name the angel, but says that the messenger told Joseph not only that Mary's conception was 'of the Holy Spirit', which would resolve some of his fears, but that he 'should not hesitate' to marry her. Perhaps this indicates that this was what Joseph wanted to do but did not quite dare to do.

The deliverer (v.21)   The name 'Joshua' or 'Jeshua' meant 'God will save', so Matthew is indulging in a play on words, but he is also indicating that Jesus came into the world to save people from their sins. Sin is the barrier between men and God; before anyone can have a true relationship with God that barrier has to be broken down. To some of Matthew's readers the phrase might have meant that Jesus would destroy the sinners, or that 'his people' included only the Jews, but the implication is that to be saved *from* something is to be set free *for* something else.

The prophecy (v.22)   This is the first example of a formula that Matthew uses some forty-eight times in his gospel: he cites Old Testament prophecies and predictions that are fulfilled in the New Testament. Probably nowhere else does the formula create so much controversy as here. Several points need to be made.

1. The quotation from Isaiah 7: 14 originally referred to a sign given to King Ahaz of Judah in about 734 B.C. as evidence of the power and presence of God. He was told that a child would be born to a 'young woman' ('almah' in Hebrew), that he would be named 'Immanuel' to show that God was with them and that before the child grew up certain pressing political problems would be solved. It is possible that Isaiah had a 'Messiah' in mind, but it is difficult to imagine that he meant anything outside his own time. The context of the prophecy, however, is also about doom and darkness being illuminated by a great light, so it is easy to see how the notes of the original got transposed into a much higher key in Christian tradition.
2. The idea that suffering was something 'inherited' from parents as a punishment for sin (e.g. John 9: 3) might have prompted Matthew to show that Jesus's later sufferings could not be blamed on any kind of sin. A virgin birth prevented that possibility.
3. Apart from the accounts of the birth in Luke and Matthew, whose differences indicate that they came from separate sources, there is no interest in the subject in any other Christian writing. This has made some wonder whether Matthew's enthusiasm for finding a text to fit the events made him seize upon this prophecy as a 'proof' of his story.
4. Although at one time it would have been considered as heresy even to harbour doubts about the birth stories, today some people regard them as 'myths' which grew up later when the gospel was preached in the Greek world, in order to give the gospel authority against traditional stories of heroes born in a miraculous manner. They also showed Jesus as having a start in life that was more fitting for his later recognition as the Son of God.

5. Whatever the division of opinion, it is clear that there are many aspects of the incarnation that we do not understand. But to Christians there is no doubt that Jesus was born, that he lived a human life on this earth and that the Holy Spirit, which is the power and presence of God, was active in all that he did and said. That he lived is a matter of fact; the rest is a matter of faith.

What is important about the birth of Jesus is not exactly what happened but what it all *means*. The birth stories are both poetic and prophetic. They form a prologue to the gospel, emphasizing the creative power of God and suggesting the dual nature of Jesus, who is at the same time both human and divine.

The decision (v.25)   Joseph, now convinced, took Mary to his home, where she became his wife. There is a belief that the marriage was never consummated and that Mary remained a virgin, but this verse seems to indicate that Joseph became her husband in more than just a legal or theoretical sense. By naming the child, Joseph was publicly acknowledging him as a member of his family.

CHAPTER 2   VISITORS AND VIOLENCE

Was Jesus really born on 25 December?   It is most unlikely. The word 'Christmas' comes from the old English 'Cristes Maesse' – 'Christ's Mass' – and according to a Roman almanac it was not celebrated on 25 December until A.D. 336. The reasons for choosing that date are very varied, but the decision seems to have been influenced mainly by the occurrence of several festivals concerned with agriculture and solar observances in midwinter, ranging from Saturnalia on 17 December to the Roman New Year on 1 January. The Christian Church decided on the 'middle' date of 25 December because it was already a feast to mark the birth date of Mithras, a god associated with the sun, and since the Messiah had been described as the 'sun of righteousness' by Malachi (4: 2) the association became obvious. However, some Eastern Churches today celebrate Christmas on other dates, including 6 January, which in the Western Church is connected with the next part of Matthew's story.

vv. 1–12   The astrologers from Persia
This story of the 'wise men' has become so surrounded by tradition and symbolism that it is now very difficult to know how to tread the path of truth with any certainty. It is a superb story, but what does it mean?

The purpose of the story   Most people, even those who profess to know the story quite well, if asked how many wise men there were, will say three, and if pressed to say why, will reply that it says so in the story. A closer examination, however, will show not only that there is no mention of how many men there were, but also that the writer gives very little detail.

Was this deliberate?   Yes, I think it was. The reason may well have been that Matthew's purpose is to present a work of art in which the value and importance of the story do not depend on those kinds of detail. In such a picture to quibble over the pigments in the paint may mean that we miss the whole point. To the writer the names or number of men or where they came from are matters of minor importance.

Then what is the point?   First, it is a missionary story, expressing the idea that men came from different lands and backgrounds to worship the Christ. Jesus is the heir to the throne of Israel, therefore it is fitting that homage should be given, not only by Jews but also by gentiles, regardless of race or religion. So we see the connection between Chapters 1 and 2 in this gospel, the deserving of honour and the receiving of it.

Secondly, it reveals the reaction of the current 'King of Jews' to this 'son of David'. Herod the Great was not a Jew or a Roman but an Idumean from the old territory of Edom. This meant that his position as ruler of Judaea, which he had held on behalf of the Romans since 40 B.C., was always precarious, for he was hated by the Jews and distrusted by the Romans. According to Flavius Josephus, the Jewish historian, Herod had ten wives and many sons and had no compunction about murdering any of them who offended him. Why a man of such treachery and cruelty should have been called 'the Great' is a mystery, unless it was because to find favour with the Jews he began to rebuild the temple in Jerusalem in 26 B.C., though he died long before it was completed.

Thirdly, to Matthew the birth story is a fulfilment of prophecy. Bethlehem – 'house of bread' – was the birthplace of King David and the prophecy in Micah 5: 2 indicated that the Messiah would be born there. Moreover, the whole story is seen as an echo of the Exodus, when the Israelites, having been exiled and enslaved in Egypt, were brought out by Moses, after the Pharaoh had killed the baby boys at the time when Moses was born. The gifts of the wise men were very similar to those in the quotation in Isaiah 60: 6, 'they from Sheba ... shall bring gold and incense'; Psalm 72: 10, 'the Kings of Sheba and Seba shall offer gifts', also anticipates this event. There seems little doubt that Matthew is either shaping the Scriptures to fit the facts or arranging his story to fit the Scriptures, although even he must have found it hard to connect Jeremiah's reference to Ramah (v. 18) with Bethlehem!

Fourthly, Matthew's is the gospel of 'the King and the Kingdom' so it is fitting that at the beginning the infant king is visited by wise men who came, as Ruskin once wrote, 'not to be curious or talkative, but to be submissive and to worship'. This 'adoration of the wise men' has inspired some of the world's greatest art because the artists, like Matthew, have seen the meaning as well as the men.

The Adoration of the Magi by Rubens

Is it right to make the story fit the scriptures in this way? Jews call this method of using stories to illustrate texts from the Bible the Midrash Haggadah. It is a traditional way of teaching the Scriptures, so Matthew would have been familiar with that method of narrating an event. But all great writers have used imagination and imagery to convey their ideas. Such are the tools of their trade and we should not try to deprive the Bible writers the use of such essential elements.

The searchers Matthew's vagueness about detail has left a vacuum which legend and tradition have not been slow to fill. It was once believed that there were seven wise men, but since the time of Tertullian (a Christian scholar writing in about A.D. 200) it has been assumed there were three because of the three gifts. Names soon followed the number – Melchior, Caspar and Balthasar – and their remains were said, for some strange reason, to rest at Cologne! Legend also gave them colours – black, brown and yellow – to indicate that they represented what were then the continents of Africa, Asia and India. Depending on which translation is used, they are referred to as wise men, magi, kings, astrologers, or even magicians!

Which definition is most likely? Many scholars think they were from Persia (Iran) and probably priests of the ancient religion Zoroastrianism, which was founded in the sixth century B.C. by the prophet Zoroaster and whose followers are now known as Parsees. If so it would explain their faith in a star, for it is a religion which takes astrology seriously and believes that great events, especially important births, are foretold by the stars. The Greek word 'magoi', from which came the Latin 'magi', means 'wise men' so possibly Matthew is suggesting that the wisdom as well as the religion of the East had come to pay tribute.

Perhaps the most important thing in Matthew's story is the characteristics of the men, not their colour or creed. They had courage and single-mindedness. They refused to abandon their aim, though we can imagine that Herod may have tried to dissuade them. Even when they were led to the most unlikely place to find a king – in a back street in Bethlehem – they may have felt at the end of their tether, but not at the end of their faith. They bowed down to the holy but not to Herod.

The star In both Matthew and Luke Jesus's birth is associated with brightness. Luke refers to the 'splendour of the Lord' which shone round the shepherds, while Matthew has the story of a star. Of course, many ancient legends contain stories of births or deaths being foretold in the stars, e.g. Cicero says that some magi saw a star which heralded the birth of Alexander the Great, so Matthew's account has a basis in tradition.

Astronomers have not yet found a satisfactory explanation to account for the star of Bethlehem, but since the Greek word that Matthew used actually means 'a luminous heavenly body' there has been no lack of suggested solutions. In 1603 the German astrologer Johannes Kepler said it was a triple conjunction of Saturn and Jupiter in the constellation of Pisces. He calculated that such a phenomenon took place every 805 years, which meant that it had occurred in 7 B.C. If the wise men had spent some time travelling – and the fact that it was a child, not a baby in the house (v. 11) may indicate that they had – then a birth date of about 6 or 5 B.C. would be probable. This is the date that scholars are generally agreed upon. (This matter is discussed further in the commentary on Luke's gospel.)

Other suggestions are that it was the morning star, since it was seen first in the east and then in the west, or Halley's Comet, which passed over that orbit in 12 B.C., although that would not fit well with the accepted birth date. An English astronomer, Dr Richard Stephenson, has carefully consulted Chinese astronomical annals and found a nova (a star that suddenly brightens, then subsides) which appeared in the spring of 5 B.C. Since we know that Herod died in 4 B.C., it follows that Jesus was born before that date.

The symbolism   Matthew is perhaps making a contrast between the 'King of the Jews' who wanted to destroy the child and the gentiles who wanted to bow down to him. There is also significance in the gifts they gave: gold was a sign of royalty; frankincense, an ingredient of holy oil used in anointing, was a sign of reverence and worship; myrrh was a fragrant resin often used to embalm the dead as well as to deaden pain, so it was symbolic of pain and death.

vv. 13–18   The sequel

The escape into Egypt seems like a retreat and a defeat, with the one who was to be the Messiah becoming a refugee! Herod's massacre of the baby boys in Bethlehem is found nowhere else in any records, not even in the writings of Josephus, whose seven books, *The Wars of the Jews*, cover the period from 175 B.C. to A.D. 70. However, it was certainly in keeping with Herod's character, which Josephus describes as 'capable, crafty and cruel'.

If Herod was so bad, why was 'all Jerusalem troubled' (v. 3) at the idea of a new king?   It does seem strange that after expecting the Messiah for hundreds of years they were now worried about his possible appearance. Surely, too, they wanted a change from Herod, or were they afraid of what he might do, since his reputation for revenge was so well known? Could it have been, perhaps, that he was not such a monster as tradition has presented him? It could also be questioned why, if he were so shrewd, he didn't send soldiers with the wise men to make sure the child was killed. Perhaps he thought that his fear would be better disguised in case it was seen as a sign of weakness.

It also seems strange that Herod, having lived among the Jews for so long, did not appear to know the prophecy (v. 5) about Bethlehem. Perhaps he wanted to check that it was the right Bethlehem, because there was another

An Arab drives his heavily laden donkey along a road outside Bethlehem

town of that name in the northern territory of Zebulun (Joshua 19: 15),
though the prophecy refers specifically to Bethlehem in Judaea.

vv. 19–23   The return from Egypt

One of the differences between the accounts in Matthew and Luke is the
original home of Joseph and Mary. According to Luke 1: 26, they lived in
Nazareth before the birth of Jesus and went to Bethlehem because of a
Roman census, returning to Nazareth afterwards (2: 39). Matthew indicates
that they already lived in or near Bethlehem and that they later went to
Nazareth in fulfilment of a prophecy (v. 23).

In this instance Matthew seems to have 'found' a prophecy which didn't
exist! He does not give any reference for it and the name 'Nazareth' is never
mentioned in the Old Testament, so there is considerable doubt as to
whether 'Nazarene' meant 'from Nazareth'. It might come from the Hebrew
word 'neser', meaning 'branch' or 'shoot', as in Isaiah 11: 1, or perhaps
from 'nasor', meaning 'preserver', as in Isaiah 49: 6. It could even come
from 'nazir', meaning 'to separate', but that would imply that Jesus was a
Nazirite, which he was not. Certainly 'Nazarene', or 'Nazorene', was a
nickname by which the followers of Jesus were known before they were
called 'Christians' (Acts 11: 26).

In any case, Galilee, under the rule of Herod's son Antipas, seemed a safer

15

place than Judaea. The latter was under the control of another son, Archelaus, who proved to be so cruel that he was removed from office in A.D. 6.

The date The visit of the magi has been celebrated on 6 January ever since the fourth century A.D. The tradition originated in the Eastern Church, where at first it included a commemoration of Christ's birth, but then the two feasts were separated. It seemed that, having decided on 25 December for the birth of Jesus, the Church had to find another date for the visit of the wise men, because it was evident from the stories that it was not immediately after the birth.

Thus, 6 January became known as Epiphany from the Greek word 'epiphaneia', meaning 'manifestation' or 'appearance'. It commemorates the first manifestation to the gentiles, represented by the wise men. In some Churches it also signifies the manifestation of Jesus's mission at his baptism.

CHAPTER 3   PREPARING THE WAY

We noted in the Introduction that this gospel contains five sections – each a collection of Jesus's teaching – and the first such section is the sermon in Chapters 5, 6 and 7. But if we regard the teaching as the nucleus of each section, we can see that the preceding chapters could be an introduction and preparation for the teaching. In this case, if the sermon is to be about the duties of and demands on those who belong to the Kingdom, Chapters 3 and 4 may be seen as leading up to that theme: John the Baptist was the king's herald, preparing the way; Jesus faces the temptations of the kingdoms offered him by the Devil; finally, he begins his mission by announcing that 'the Kingdom is at hand'.

vv. 1–12   The desert preacher   (Mark 1: 1–8, Luke 3: 1–20)
Matthew says that John the Baptist 'appeared as a preacher in the Judaean wilderness', an area to the west of the Dead Sea. This may sound as though John was a solitary recluse, though that was not so. Later on (11: 11) Jesus is to describe him as 'greater than anyone who has ever lived' so he must have had qualities which marked him out as more than just a messenger. Of course, Matthew is anxious to liken John to Elijah, who had also appeared on the scene very suddenly as a preacher and a prophet (1 Kings 17: 1).

vv. 1–6   The declaration
All four gospels tell of John's sudden appearance, to speak the prologue, as it were, and to prepare the way for the Messiah, but they describe it rather differently. Mark links John's appearance with what he says is a quotation from Isaiah, but which in fact is a mixture of Isaiah 40: 1–3 and Malachi 3: 1. He then goes on to describe his dress and his diet of 'locusts and wild honey'. Luke and John give no details of his appearance but instead

16

concentrate on John's criticism of the religious leaders and his reply to their questions. Matthew combines Mark and Luke, though he spots Mark's mistake about Malachi and gives only the genuine Isaiah passage.

The shores of the Dead Sea

'*About that time*' (v. 1)   Matthew's phrase is very vague but according to Luke 3: 23, Jesus was 'about thirty years of age' when he began to preach, so John would have been the same age.

'*Repent*' (v. 2)   The Greek word literally means 'a change of mind', which indicates that John was demanding much more than a passive 'being sorry for sins'. He was asking for real remorse for past sins and a positive determination to change direction completely, as far as their present life and future outlook were concerned. In fact, some scholars point out that John's baptizing was similar to that required of converts to Judaism, which might explain why some of the crowd were not convinced of their need for such a ceremony. It is worth noting, however, that Jews themselves practise immersion as an act of renewal and refreshment.

Why was John living in the wilderness?   Luke (1: 80) tells us that John 'lived out in the wilds' until he appeared as a preacher. This may mean that he joined a religious order living at Qumran, at the north-west end of the Dead Sea, who are thought to have been the 'Essenes'. Nowhere in the New Testament are they actually mentioned by name, but Josephus mentions the sect in his *Wars of the Jews*, calling them 'Essenoi', which may come from the Greek word 'hosioi', meaning 'holy', or from the ancient Syriac word 'hasya', meaning 'pious'.

There are certainly many similarities between John's preaching and the sect's 'manual' of discipline. For example, they believed that certain men should be 'set apart to prepare a way in the wilderness for our God', and they also had specific rules for ceremonial washing and immersion and for the sharing of food and possessions. Excavations have led many scholars to believe that these Essenes were responsible for writing the documents found in the Qumran caves in 1947 and now known as 'The Dead Sea Scrolls'.

vv. 7–12   The demands

The words of John the Baptist are the same in Matthew and Luke, but while Luke says (3: 7) that they were directed to 'the crowds', Matthew singles out the Pharisees and Sadducees.

Who were these religious leaders?
The Pharisees   The word, from the Hebrew 'parush' and the Aramaic 'perisha', literally meant 'separated ones'. There are a number of possible reasons for this name. One is that the Pharisees tended to keep themselves 'apart' from other people. By their observance of rules about ceremonial purity they separated themselves not only from non-Jews but also from many of their fellow Jews who were less strict in outlook. The Sabbath in particular was surrounded with what seemed to many to be unreasonable restrictions. It was this practice that Jesus often objected to. Another possibility is that the name derived from the Pharisees' 'separateness' from state politics.

The Pharisees believed in angels and life after death and, unlike the Sadducees, accepted certain unwritten laws or 'traditions' as well as the written law. Their origins probably went back to the time when the Jews returned from exile in Babylon in 539–8 B.C., but the actual sect of 'Pharisees' is first mentioned in the time of the High Priest Hyrcanus (135–104 B.C.).

The Sadducees   A smaller sect than the Pharisees, they came chiefly from the wealthy upper classes of the priesthood. In fact, Josephus tells us that all the high-priestly families belonged to the Sadducee sect. Their name probably came from Zadok, the High Priest in David's time (2 Samuel 8: 17), since the Greek word for Zadok was 'Saddouk', though this is not certain. They took the written law very literally and had little time for the Pharisees' more liberal interpretations, so the two parties were often hostile towards each other. After the fall of Jerusalem in A.D. 70 the party seems to have disappeared.

Surely v. 7 means that they came to John together?   Not necessarily. They could have come from different directions or from a common fear of the coming judgement. It has been suggested that their coming together in v. 7 meant that they had made a truce in order to oppose the man whose preaching seemed to undermine their own position and policies.

The denunciations   Whatever their reasons for coming, they were greeted with some cutting comments when they arrived! Calling people vipers is hardly complimentary, nor is it likely to win their co-operation. 'Having Abraham for our father' didn't merely mean that they were Jews, but also implied a belief that keeping the law strictly was some kind of insurance policy against the fires of judgement. John also indulged in an ironic play on words (v. 9) to make his point: the Aramaic word for 'stones' was 'ebhanim', while the word for 'children' was 'banim'.

So, he said, the Messiah was coming to sort out people on a grand scale and in no uncertain fashion, with the 'trees' of tradition not only being cut down (v. 10) but the roots dug up as well. John referred to himself as just a servant, not fit to unfasten the Messiah's sandals, but he likened the one who would come after him to a farmer tossing up the corn into the air on a windy day so that the chaff would blow away and the grain would remain. It was going to be an upheaval that would bring as much hardship as healing.

Wouldn't John be more likely to antagonize people than attract them?   It is a fair question to ask whether John was suitable as forerunner to the Messiah. Everything about him was startling – his appearance, his attitude and his actions. The words of Isaiah 40, from which John quoted, begin with a message of comfort and go on to express the hope that the rough places will be made plain. But John's manner seemed more conducive to separation than smoothness, and conflict rather than comfort. It seemed that, except for those who were ready to delight in some kind of divine judgement, all the talk of fires and axes would be an obstacle rather than a help, as far as religious belief was concerned.

But John's role was that of a reformer and such a person is not always popular. His message would be good news to those who wanted genuine change, but unwelcome to those who wanted to enter God's Kingdom without any real repentance.

vv. 13–17 John's dilemma (Mark 1: 9–11, Luke 3: 21–22)

According to Mark only Jesus was baptized by John, but Luke says that it was during a 'general baptism of the people'. Matthew makes it clear (v. 13) that Jesus had come specifically to be baptized by John, but then voices the question which he knew his readers would raise: if baptism was for the washing away of sin and a public sign of private repentance, why was Jesus baptized? Surely it should have been Jesus who baptized John! It was this habit of anticipating questions that made Matthew a favourite gospel in the early Church.

To John's objection Jesus gave an answer which varies according to the translation used. The Jerusalem Bible, for example, has 'Leave it like this for the time being. It is fitting that we should, in this way, do all that righteousness demands.'

What did that mean? It is not certain, but some suggestions can be made.
1. 'Righteousness', in the Bible, especially the Psalms, often meant that God was just in carrying out his promises and prophecies. Here it could refer to the prophecies in Psalm 2: 7 and Isaiah 42: 1 about an anointed king and the 'servant of the Lord', both of which are implied in a 'voice from heaven', mentioned by Matthew in v. 17. The Hebrew term 'bath qol' meant 'daughter of a voice' and was used to refer to a message from God.
2. Jesus wanted to associate himself with John's mission and movement, not stand apart as a spectator.
3. The baptism was not only a focal point, but also a turning-point in the life of Jesus. It was a clearing of his mind and a confirmation of what God wanted him to do. It was what the prophets would have described as a 'call' to serve God, a commission to obey God's commands. Perhaps that is why the baptism was later referred to as Jesus's 'illumination'.
4. It has been pointed out that 'Messiah' and 'son' do not mean the same thing. Possibly Jesus had been aware of his Messiahship, but now his 'sonship' was also confirmed.

What was the dove (v. 16)? The image of a dove is used many times in the Bible. It is usually a gentle and timid creature and Jesus refers to it (Matthew 10: 16) as 'harmless'. Here it is a symbol representing the Spirit of God, just as in Genesis 1: 2 the Spirit is represented as 'hovering' over the waters like a bird. Also, perhaps Matthew had in mind that the 'Spirit' in the first creation story in Genesis brought light out of darkness.

Jesus's preaching ministry had not yet begun. The baptism may have clarified certain issues and given a clear call for Jesus to begin his work, but it must also have caused conflict in his mind as to what his role as the 'Messiah' really meant. What did being the 'beloved son' signify and how was he to present the idea of God's Kingdom to people whose popular expectation of a Messiah was one who would set up a political kingdom and restore the nation to its former greatness? Jesus needed time and solitude to clear his mind and discover the way to fulfil his mission. We call this experience 'The Temptations'.

Why call them that? We nearly always associate the word with enticement to do wrong, but the examples given here seem almost disguised as ways of doing good, which is how temptation sometimes appears. Of course there were many different beliefs about how the Messiah should behave and the part he should play in the religious and political life of the nation. Jesus had decided what he had to do, but now he had to consider how to fulfil his vocation, despite the demands from various sources for him to act differently.

The tempter The word 'devil' comes from the Greek 'diabolos', which really means 'slanderer' and is a term usually found in later New Testament writings rather than the gospels. Mark (1: 12) prefers the Old Testament description 'Satan', which meant 'adversary', as in Job 1: 6, where Satan roamed over the earth, causing as much chaos as he possibly could. In the Bible as a whole he dons many disguises, ranging from a serpent in the second creation story (Genesis 3), to 'a roaring lion seeking whom he may devour' (1 Peter 5: 8), and even an enemy carrying off the wheat seed (Matthew 13: 19).

The territory The 'wilderness', which is mentioned often in the Bible, was the area on the western side of the Dead Sea. It was very hot and barren and often thought of as the home of evil spirits.

The time Forty is a significant number in Judaism, often used to indicate a length of time associated with expectation or waiting. After the Exodus the Israelites journeyed for forty years in the wilderness and Moses fasted for forty days and nights (Exodus 34: 28) before writing down the Commandments. The phrase 'forty days' is often used to indicate a long time rather than a specific period. Today the forty days Jesus spent in the wilderness are represented by the period known as Lent, which begins on Ash Wednesday and ends on Easter Eve: excluding Sundays, this period is forty days.

vv. 1–11 The temptations (Mark 1: 12–13, Luke 4: 1–13)
Mark, though giving no details, says that Jesus was tempted *during* the forty

The 'wilderness' to the west of the Dead Sea

days of fasting, while Matthew and Luke imply that the temptations came *after* the fasting. They both get their information from 'Q', but use it in a slightly different order.

The story must have originally come from Jesus himself, as he described his experience in dramatic form to the disciples. One suggestion is that he did so after Peter's confession (Matthew 16: 13) when the whole question of Messiahship was probably discussed.

Was the devil real? Some think he was, but others see the story as symbolic. Picture language is probably being used to convey the conflict that went on in Jesus's mind.

Was the number three significant? Like forty it has special importance, often to indicate a repetition of events. It is interesting to note that today, when people give examples of something or illustrate a point, they often use three as the most suitable number. In the case of these temptations, it seems as though they were a pointer towards the kinds of issue that Jesus would face. They have also been described as the three forms in which temptation comes most strongly to many people: the appeal to self-interest, the inclination towards self-preservation and protection, and the desire for influence and power.

22

1. Bread and bribery   (vv. 2–4)

This was a temptation because it was an attempt to get Jesus to use his miraculous powers to provide for himself and to satisfy his hunger after the stringent self-discipline of fasting. The temptor was saying, 'If you are the son of God, prove it by giving a demonstration of your power.'

It was also an attractive idea to go and feed others. People in Palestine were often on the breadline, so anyone who could give them food would be worth following. But the temptation was to give people *only* bread, to satisfy their physical needs but not their spiritual and moral requirements.

It was rejected because Jesus's miraculous powers were not for his own glory or gratification. He had accepted human life and must accept its limitations in the same way that, like everyone else, he must trust God for his daily bread. But perhaps most important, although feeding people was not wrong, it was not enough. People need faith and forgiveness as well as food. The mind and the soul must also be fed.

That is why this temptation was withstood with the words from Deuteronomy 8: 3, 'Man cannot live by bread alone'.

2. Trust and towers   (vv. 5–7)

The 'Holy City' was of course Jerusalem. Its Arabic name, 'El-Quds', means 'holy'. The pinnacle or parapet was a tower on the south side of the temple which Josephus describes as 'a dizzy height' and from which there was a tremendous drop down into the valley below.

It was a temptation in complete contrast to the first. The first had implied a doubt that God could provide food, here it was assumed that God *would* provide some kind of protective power if Jesus jumped from the tower. It would also attract the attention and allegiance of those who would see it as fulfilment of the prophecy about the Messiah 'coming down on the clouds of heaven' (Daniel 7: 13).

Moreover, Psalm 91, believed by many Jews to be Messianic, said that the one who trusted God would be kept safe from harm, as the devil quoted (v. 6). So why not put such a promise of protection to the test and ask God to show proof of Jesus's sonship in this special way?

This was rejected because such an action would be testing God instead of trusting him. That is why Jesus's reply, again from Deuteronomy (6: 16), was a reference to the Israelites blaming Moses when they had no water in the wilderness and doubted whether God was with them or not. Moses had named the place 'Massah', which meant 'to challenge' or 'to tempt'.

Besides, being God's son didn't mean being excused from suffering. Serving God was not an insurance policy against pain and hardship. If Jesus had jumped and been miraculously saved the watching crowd would no doubt have been impressed by such a demonstration of divine deliverance, but for how long? Followers had to be won by goodness, not by gimmicks.

23

3. Kingdoms and compromises (vv. 8–10)

Matthew probably leaves this one until last because he sees it as the most subtle. The temptor drops the 'if you are God's son' approach and gets down to the question of political power. It could also refer to a matter of importance to the Jews: the gaining of freedom from Rome and the setting up of a Jewish kingdom.

The 'very high mountain' (v. 8) is no doubt Matthew's way of reminding the reader about Moses on Mount Sinai and also on Mount Nebo as he looked out over the Promised Land. Today tradition associates the 'Mount of Temptation' with a flat-topped mountain near Jericho, overlooking the wilderness.

It was a temptation because the Jews in the Roman empire longed for a leader to help them shake off the shackles of Rome and set up their own kingdom. Such a leader would command widespread support. Moreover, the prophecies had spoken of such a leader (e.g. Isaiah 11: 1–5), so provided that the end was good, did it matter about the means used to achieve it?

It was an appeal to 'holy ambition'. The devil said, 'All this I will give you, if you will worship me', so why not compromise with him and then use this 'territory' for a better purpose? Surely the essential things were social justice and being seen to be a 'man of the people'? Wasn't there a time when politics had to take priority over morality if a person wished to remain a popular preacher?

It was rejected because such a compromise was simply a means of taking a short cut to success and popularity. It would be an abuse not a use of power. To be identified with those who wanted to establish an earthly kingdom by force and fighting would be not reform but revolution. To put politics before principles might make the headlines, but it wouldn't really be good news.

So the reply, from Deuteronomy 6: 13–14, was a reminder that a true relationship with God meant absolute allegiance, not an apparent service which was only spare-time.

'The devil left him' (v. 11) does not mean that he never returned or that the temptations never recurred. Luke says the devil 'left him for a while', which implies that he came back later and that the temptations, in another form, were repeated. For example, according to John's gospel (6: 15), after the feeding of the five thousand the crowd wanted Jesus to be their leader and presumably start some kind of revolt against the Romans.

vv. 12–17 The mission begins (Mark 1: 14–15, Luke 4: 14–15)

Whatever the reason for John's arrest – and some believe that it was the work of those who wanted him out of the way – the 'forerunner' had been removed and must now be replaced. According to the synoptic gospels, Jesus and John did not overlap in their preaching, but the fourth gospel, which does not mention John's arrest or his death, indicates that they did overlap.

All three synoptics say that Jesus went to Galilee to begin his ministry, but they emphasize different details of the way it started. Luke tells of the preaching in the synagogue at Nazareth (Ch. 4), while Mark wastes no time in telling how Jesus preached about the Kingdom of God (1: 15). Matthew finds a quotation to suit the occasion, though in this case it does not entirely fit the narrative since in the Old Testament the territory of Zebulun lay between Galilee and the coast, so it would almost certainly not have included Capernaum, though the territory of Naphtali might possibly have extended that far. Moreover, his quotation differs from the original (Isaiah 9: 1–2). But his main point is to show that even these 'despised' regions could share in the blessings and be brought to the light, so he is using the prophecy to explain why Jesus went to work in 'lowly' Galilee, rather than Judaea.

Matthew also says that Jesus left Nazareth to live in Capernaum, which no other gospel mentions. Perhaps this was because the people in Nazareth failed to respond (Mark 6: 1–6).

Capernaum – 'village of Nahum' – is almost certainly the present-day 'Tell Hum', on the northern shore of the lake. It is now nothing more than a ruin, but then it was a busy commercial centre.

Was that the best place to begin his ministry?   In one sense it was an odd choice because it was not a religious centre and was much better known for

The shores of Lake Galilee

25

its work than for its worship, but in another sense it was an ideal starting-place, because it was a town which showed greater tolerance towards new ideas than some other areas elsewhere.

'Galil' means 'circle' and Galilee consisted of a circle of towns around the lake. 'Galilee of the Gentiles' originally meant a 'region of non-Jews', to some people a 'land of darkness', but a land which needed the light of Jesus's preaching.

The opening words (v. 17) Like the Baptist, Jesus began with a request to repent. A Hebrew word often used in this context means 'to grieve for one's sins'. What was needed was a genuine sorrow for past sins and a resolution not to repeat them.

Matthew uses the phrase 'the Kingdom of Heaven' rather than 'the Kingdom of God', used by Mark and Luke, perhaps to avoid mentioning God's name. The phrase is not actually found in the Old Testament, but the expectation of the reign or sovereignty of God on earth was implied in many of the prophecies and in the apocalyptic (meaning 'revealed') literature such as Joel and Daniel. In the latter case, however, many believed it to have political and revolutionary overtones. Jesus said that the Kingdom was 'now near', indicating that his ministry would show what it really was.

vv. 18–22 The ordinary men (Mark 1: 16–20, Luke 5: 1–11)

The account of how Jesus chose certain men to be his 'students', which is what the word 'disciples' means, varies in all four gospels. Matthew follows Mark fairly closely, but Luke gives different details, omitting Andrew from the four, while John (1: 35–42) implies that Andrew and Simon, at least, were disciples of John the Baptist before they became followers of Jesus.

At the time the men were catching fish, but Jesus told them that in future they would 'catch men'. In Jeremiah 16: 16–18 that phrase implied hunting someone in order to bring them to justice, to 'face the consequences', but here Jesus uses the term in the sense of saving others *from* the consequences of evil.

Why did he choose fishermen? Principally because he saw the potential they possessed. Most rabbis in those days had 'disciples', whom they taught about the law and its interpretation, but Jesus wanted his disciples to go out and teach. Jesus didn't choose his men because they were particularly pious or wealthy or well educated, but because they possessed the kind of qualities he was looking for. They were men of patience, courage and common sense. They were not perfect but they had great possibilities. So he took them on as they were, because he would make them into what he wanted them to be. For their part, they saw in Jesus the sort of man for whom the sacrifice of leaving so much behind was worthwhile.

St Augustine summed it up neatly when he said, 'These men did not forsake their nets – they simply used them for another purpose.'

vv. 23–25   The beginning of the ministry   (Luke 6: 17–19)

Luke begins the account of Jesus's public ministry (Ch. 4) on a note of opposition, but Matthew gives a more positive view of Jesus's initial work. On his tour of the synagogues in Galilee it seemed that Jesus was so popular that people came from as far afield as Syria and Judaea to hear him, though it is possible that some of the interest owed more to the curing of illness than the preaching of a prophet.

A synagogue (v.23) was to be found in every village, since it needed only a community of ten males to set one up. It was a continuation of an institution begun in the Exile in Babylon, when the Jews, not having a temple, formed local places for worship, study and meeting. When they went back to their homeland they took the idea with them, though the synagogue soon assumed a much wider purpose than just a place of worship. It was also a school, a meeting-house and a local council. In the services, at which a visitor might be invited to speak, there was sometimes an interpreter to translate the Hebrew of the Scriptures into the local Aramaic dialect.

Matthew uses this short section on the beginning of Jesus's ministry as an introduction to what many see not only as the most fascinating feature of this gospel, but also as one of the greatest discourses on moral principles in all ethical teaching.

THE SOUL-SEARCHING SERMON
CHAPTERS 5, 6, 7 (Luke 6: 17–49)

This is the nucleus of the first section of Matthew's gospel and, to many people, the heart of the whole Christian religion. They contend that if all else were lost and only these chapters survived we should still be left with the foundation stones of the Christian faith.

Luke gives the location of this sermon as 'on level ground' but Matthew says that Jesus 'went up the hill' (5: 1) which is why it is known as 'The Sermon on the Mount'.

Why the difference?   In the Old Testament mountains had a special significance as far as God's revelation was concerned (e.g. Elijah on Carmel, 1 Kings 18: 37–38), and there seems little doubt here that Matthew had in mind Moses receiving the Ten Commandments on Mount Sinai (Exodus 19). When he says 'the hill' (v. 5) he may have had a particular one in mind, but the place is not of great significance. What Matthew wants to show is the importance of the teaching and the fact that just as Moses received the Law on a mountain, Jesus is giving a new Law, also on a mountain. To Luke there is no need for such a setting: he sees the teaching as more 'down to earth'.

The composition   Few scholars think that the sermon was delivered all at one sitting. Jesus was too wise a teacher to spoil such a good moral 'meal' by giving his hearers mental indigestion. It is a collection of sayings, advice, illustrations and ethical truths given on different occasions, possibly some of it from synagogue sermons by Jesus and remembered by some of the more receptive listeners. Most of the material almost certainly comes from 'Q', though the way in which Matthew and Luke each uses the material may mean that there was more than one version of that document. Some scholars believe that Luke's account is the original nucleus, which Matthew expanded.

The purpose Matthew sees the sermon as meeting a need. Jesus was going to delegate some of the preaching and teaching to the men he had chosen and they would need some guide-lines for their own lives and for their relationships with other people. According to Matthew, Jesus addressed the disciples but since Matthew has so far told of the choosing of only four, we can assume that the teaching was in fact meant for a much wider audience.

Just as the writer has divided his gospel into five sections, so the sermon can also be divided into five parts.

CHAPTER 5
Part 1

vv. 3–12   The recipe for real happiness
These verses are known as the 'Beatitudes', from the Latin 'beatitudo', meaning 'blessedness'. There are plenty of examples of the same idea in the Psalms, e.g. 32: 1, 41: 1. Some translations begin with 'how blest...', others have 'happy are...', while some suggest 'how fortunate...' or even 'congratulations to...'.

Some scholars, perhaps deducing that Matthew is making a new 'decalogue' (Ten Commandments), say there are ten Beatitudes, with verse 12 as the tenth, but there appear to be only nine. It doesn't matter. The vital thing is that they contain a code for true happiness, as long as it is remembered that such a state of mind is not just a sense of well-being, but results from a particular way of life.

1. *The lowly* (v. 3)   Luke simply says 'the poor', Matthew adds 'in spirit' from Psalm 34: 18. Whatever translation is used, it means people who are the opposite of arrogant. They have a divine discontent in the sense that they know they fall far short of God's demands. In that sense they are 'poor'. It is not that they live in poverty, though some may, but that they have lost the pride which so often keeps a person from entering the Kingdom.

2. *The sorrowful* (v. 4)   Some versions say 'mourn', but it is not referring to those who have lost a loved one. It means those who are saddened by the sin and sorrow they see in the world and long for it to be a better place, just as a bereaved person longs to see a loved one again. Such sorrow will find 'comfort', which does not mean just consolation (though some modern

translations use this weaker word), but the giving of strength to the weak and a challenge to the complacency of those who are indifferent.

3. *The gentle* (v. 5)   Some translations have 'meek', which is open to misunderstanding. Meekness is not weakness, nor is gentleness just being inoffensive. The original Greek word means 'reverent obedience'. The phrase comes from Psalm 37: 11, where the word is 'humble'. Moses is described as being 'meek above all men' (Numbers 12: 3), but that didn't mean he was indecisive.

There is nothing negative about this beatitude. A person who is not resentful and bears no grudge and who does not want to inflict suffering on anyone else has positive qualities. They may not possess very much in the material sense, but they possess a peace of mind which is the most valuable thing on earth.

4. *The hungry* (v. 6)   Again, Matthew is referring to a mental not a physical state. He knew very well that there is nothing holy about being hungry, but he meant that people should have a moral hunger to see goodness generated and truth and morality defended. It is not those who merely feel 'that there is something wrong with the world' who will be satisfied; it is those who know they have done their utmost to remedy the wrongs. Perhaps Jesus had a verse from Proverbs in mind (21: 21): 'Persevere in right conduct and you will find life'.

5. *The merciful* (v. 7)   This means much more than being charitable or simply sentimental. It does not just mean forgetting a wrong or an injury, it means there should be a deep compassion which comes from a real delight in kindness. It is a 'mercy' that springs not from a feeling of superiority but from a knowledge that everyone stands in need of forgiveness. Such an attitude, as Shakespeare said (Merchant of Venice, IV, i), 'blesses him that gives and him that takes', and such people can expect mercy in return.

6. *The honest* (v. 8)   To be 'pure in heart' means more than just having a clean mind and refusing to reduce all human relationships to a very low level. The word 'heart', when used in the Bible, means personality and character, the mind as well as the emotions. A 'pure heart' in Psalm 24: 4 means that a person had not 'set his mind on falsehood', and the word 'pure', which occurs some twenty-eight times in the New Testament, means pureness of motive as well as of mind.

Such people 'see God' in the sense that they see his goodness when others see only despair.

7. *The peacemakers* (v. 9)   This does not mean those who merely throw up their hands in horror at the thought of war or compromise to avoid conflict at any cost. It means those who actively 'seek peace and pursue it' (Psalm 34: 14). This is not passive, it is preventive. It gets to the root of the troubles which create tension and deals with the symptoms before they develop into

29

the disease. Sometimes so-called 'peace' is only exhausted hatred. To *make* peace is hard work and means involvement, not running away from responsibilities. Such people are co-workers with Christ and therefore God's 'children'.

8. & 9.   *The persecuted* (vv. 10–11)   Some say that vv. 10 and 11 are the same and therefore there are only eight Beatitudes, but there is a subtle difference between them. One is in the past tense and one in the future, so it sounds as though verse 11 was addressed specifically to the disciples who were to suffer 'insults and persecution' later on. Here it seems to refer to real hostility and it might well be asked what is 'blessed' about being persecuted! But the essential thing is the reason for the persecution. Here it is 'for the cause of right' and in verse 11 it is 'for my sake'. To suffer criticism and opposition in such causes is no disgrace. People often tend to persecute someone who offers a challenge to their particular way of life.

The praise (v. 12)   This could be regarded as the tenth Beatitude, though it is more like a benedictus: 'don't be down hearted, rejoice and be glad'. To be called upon to suffer for one's faith is to follow a long line of witnesses. Certainly, prophets like Jeremiah, Ezekiel and Amos were subjected to all kinds of ill-treatment.

vv. 13–16   Essential ingredients
'Salt' and 'light' were no trivial items. Salt was valued for many reasons, principally as a preservative and an appetizer, but also as an investment, since a bag of salt was reckoned as precious as a man's life and it could always command a good price and a high rate of taxation. The danger was that it would become damp or adulterated (mixed with another substance), then it would lose its value.

Light has always been a mystery, but always recognized as something without which there could be no life or growth. In the Bible light is always used as a symbol for goodness and truthfulness, while darkness is a symbol for evil and despair. In John's gospel (8: 12) Jesus describes himself as the 'light of the world'; here he says that those who try to embrace the Beatitudes will also be like light, to help and guide other people. But even light can lose its power and purpose if it is hidden or prevented from shining. Followers of Jesus must spread goodness as a lamp sheds light.

Part 2

vv. 17–48   New laws for old
In this second section of the sermon Matthew gives some examples of the old and new laws, the contrast between the Laws given to the Israelites through Moses and the demands that Jesus made. In his introduction (vv. 17–20), however, he makes it quite clear that Jesus was not saying that the Laws of Moses no longer mattered, but that he was giving them a new

meaning. He had come not to condemn the Laws but to complete them and to give them a wider signficance.

The smallest Greek letter was 'iota' and the smallest Hebrew character was 'yod', so even the tiniest detail of the Law was important (v. 18), but to 'complete' it meant to keep it in mind as well as in deed. To refrain from doing wrong is not enough; it is important not to *want* to do wrong. To keep a law simply from fear of being found out or punished is one thing, but to keep it out of consideration for others and a sense of justice is another. In the first instance the letter of the law is kept, in the second the spirit of the law.

So Jesus was taking a new look at the Law and giving new depth to its demands. Matthew gives several examples.

vv. 21–26 Murder

One can just imagine the consternation when Jesus quoted the sixth commandment (Exodus 20) and then said, 'But I tell you this...'. Moses had been given the Laws on Mount Sinai and these had held good for more than a thousand years, but now a young 'nobody' from Nazareth was saying he could supersede them!

But his point was clear. To keep that commandment in deed is not very difficult, but to feel virtuous for not actually hitting anyone over the head is false piety. What if there is a desire to do harm and a hatred and contempt which may lead to crime unless it is controlled? Only when there is no wish to hurt anyone can someone be said to have 'completed' the Law.

Is Jesus saying that the thought is as bad as the deed?   No, he is not placing them in the same category. One is open and one is hidden. People are not committed to prison for what is only in their minds, but many murders are the result of anger and hatred and to examine the cause is often to avoid the consequences.

'The fires of hell' (v. 22)   The phrase is a combination of two Jewish ideas on the place of the dead and the place of burning. The Hebrew 'Sheol' and the Greek 'Haides' were names for the dark gloomy underworld of the dead. The Hebrew 'Ge' hinnom' referred to the valley of Hinnom just outside Jerusalem where human sacrifices had once been practised and where the rubbish was burnt. The name became associated with burning, and from it came the Latin 'Gehenna', meaning a place of punishment.

vv. 27–30 Adultery

Again, the seventh commandment condemned the physical act, but Jesus referred to the lust which was like committing the act in imagination. Self-discipline had gone and self-indulgence taken over.

The word was usually applied to sexual relations between a man and a married woman who was not his wife and the punishment was harsh for both offenders (Leviticus 20: 10). In a general sense it meant immorality and unfaithfulness.

The 'mutilations' mentioned in vv. 29–30 are of course an exaggeration, but they make the point dramatically.

vv. 31–32 Divorce (Mark 10: 11–12, Luke 16: 18)

'They were told' refers to Deuteronomy 24: 1, although the law was really an attempt to clarify the woman's position and status, since after the certificate had been given to the wife it could not be retracted. The woman could not divorce her husband, but she could go to court to demand that he divorce her, if she felt he was making her life unbearable.

In those days there were two schools of thought on the matter – Rabbi Hillel said the husband could divorce his wife for any reason, whilst Rabbi Shammai said it could be only for a serious matter such as adultery and unfaithfulness. That may explain Jesus's reply (v. 32), although some scholars believe that the phrase 'except for unchastity' is Matthew's own addition and that Jesus himself was making no exceptions.

Was Jesus saying that divorce for any reason is wrong? Perhaps not, but I think he was saying that marriage is a contract and a commitment, not a mere convenience. It is a coming together of minds, bodies and personalities and it should be a sacrament showing how the love of God can be reflected in the relationships between human beings. When that respect and love is gone, there is very little left.

vv. 33–37 Promises

This quotation was not a specific commandment, but a summary of several different passages about making promises in God's name, i.e. Leviticus 19: 12 and Deuteronomy 23: 21, as well as the third commandment about taking God's name in vain. It was really a matter of a promise being binding. If a person meant what he said why make him swear an oath? Did that mean that he was not trustworthy?

Usually an oath entailed using God's name, but other expressions, such as 'by heaven and earth', could be used, though these were less emphatic. Jesus condemned the use of oaths, saying that a person's word should be his bond and should not need to be sworn.

Today some religious sects interpret the words to mean that even taking an oath in court is forbidden, so they refuse to do so.

vv. 38–42 Hitting back (Luke 6: 27–36)

To most Jews – and to many other people – the Biblical law on revenge seemed reasonable. The original quotation (Exodus 21: 23–25) also included 'Life for life, hand for hand and bruise for bruise', as well as eyes and teeth. The laws of Moses, Babylon and Rome all stipulated that a wrongdoer should be punished in proportion to the offence. Surely retaliation of the exact amount was better than indiscriminate revenge on whole families or peoples?

Jesus offered a different approach. The fact that a person had done someone a wrong did not mean that the latter should retaliate. Jesus was not advocating a feeble giving way to aggression, but putting forward a positive way of stopping the trouble spreading. If someone hits another across the face the most natural reaction is to hit back, but a more difficult thing to do is to refuse to retaliate, not through cowardice but through strength. Of course, Jesus was speaking of the response of an individual against what was done to that person. How far such actions can be decided on behalf of someone else is very debatable.

If a Roman soldier forced a Jew, as they often did, to carry his pack from one Roman milestone to the next – about 1500 metres – and the Jew instead of then throwing the pack in the road offered to carry it a further mile, the soldier might think he was strange. However, it was possible that at the end of the extra mile they might part friends!

vv. 43–48   Love and hatred

Leviticus 19: 18 certainly said 'you shall love your neighbour as yourself', but there was no mention of hating enemies. Perhaps the 'hatred' was implied rather than expressed, though the word 'hate' in the Semitic idiom could mean 'to love less'. This could have the negative meaning of doing someone no harm; by contrast, Jesus was demanding positive action.

The Greek word used here for 'love' – 'agape' – does not mean emotional or family love, but a concern for the welfare of others, even those who are not very lovable. In that sense one can try to love enemies. To love family and friends is easy enough, but to love other people is sometimes more difficult.

Yet God has no favourites. He does not discriminate: the rain and the sun – and presumably the floods and the drought – affect good and bad alike.

The tax-collectors (v. 47) are singled out for special mention because many of them were noted for their narrowness in looking after only their own interests and caring only for those who could pay them well. They were also hated because they colluded with the Roman oppressors. Perhaps Jesus had in mind the 'telonai', the 'lower grade' collectors, who were hated even more than the 'publicani', the higher-ranking ones.

'Father' (v.48) occurs seventeen times in this sermon, showing how Jesus wanted to emphasize the fact that all people are children of God. The translation of 'You must be perfect' in one version of the New English Bible as 'There must be no limit to your goodness' is appropriate because the Greek word Matthew uses means 'that which is at the end'. It is something to strive for and struggle to achieve.

Isn't all this more theoretical than practical?   There has always been a tendency to think that Jesus did not mean this sermon to be taken literally. Many have protested that such teaching is not only unrealistic but would mean the breakdown of all social order. So it is said that he was talking about some kind of future ideal society or he was setting such a high standard that people should be driven to repentance when they realized how inadequate they were. But why did he say these things if they were not to be taken seriously? Just because a standard is very high does not mean that it should not be aimed at, even though meeting the demands made in the sermon may seem impossible.

CHAPTER 6

Part 3

vv. 1–18   Pretence and practice

Matthew's third section deals with the difference between doing good things for show or personal satisfaction and doing them purely for God's sake and the benefit of others. There is always a danger that 'doing good' can degenerate into a means of self-satisfaction, to be seen by as many spectators as possible. It is a common human failing. Real goodness should be a secret solely between the individual and God.

Several examples are given.

vv. 1–4   Generosity

The important thing is a person's motive for giving to a good cause. Almsgiving was – and still is – an important part of Jewish religious life, but sometimes the reasons could be wrong. To some people it may have been not simply a way of helping the poor, but also a good 'investment' for some kind of reward in a future life. It was also sometimes a way of impressing other people, who would observe what a good man Mr So-and-so was!

In the Apocryphal book of Tobit (12: 9) it says, 'Alms rescues from death and will cleanse from all sin', but a desire to be *seen* doing good can spoil the giving.

The act   The 'flourish of trumpets' could mean the hiring of a trumpeter to draw attention to the giving, but more probably it refers to the practice of trumpets being sounded on occasions such as fast days, when money was given to the poor; this could be used as an opportunity to win admiration.

The actors   The word 'hypocrite' had several meanings, including 'an interpreter of dreams'. The original Greek word meant 'one who plays a part'. In the Greek theatre it was common for actors to wear a mask, which hid their real identity.

The attitude   When someone gives for personal glory, the reward is instant: people notice and nod approval. The word used here literally means 'receipt'. Real giving, however, does not demand any recognition, it is a secret between God and the giver.

Prayer is very important to Jews. Here prayers are being said on the coast of Israel at the Tashlich ceremony during the Jewish New Year.

vv. 5–15 Prayers

Jesus was not criticizing the practice of prayer, but the way in which it was sometimes carried out. Three times a day prayers were said, either at home or outside in the open or in the synagogue. The 'babbling' (v. 7) could be derived from a nickname sometimes given to an orator who bored his audience, or it could come from an Aramaic word meaning 'to stammer'. The Roman writer Seneca (4 B.C. – A.D. 65), in his *Epistles*, complained of people who 'tire out the gods with words'.

The personal prayer (vv. 9–13)   A good prayer has been described as 'giving one's mind to God'. To do that, the prayer should be simple and sincere, and should not allow any distractions. To illustrate the kind of prayer he had in mind, Jesus gave his followers a model prayer. He did not say, 'Use these exact words and no others'; what has become known as the Lord's Prayer is really a model on which all daily devotions should be based, a pattern for all petitions to God.

Luke's version of the prayer (11: 2–4) is shorter and some think it is the original form, possibly used at the ceremony of baptism, with Matthew's being used in general church worship. The prayer is an example of the 'Q' source. Very similar phrases are found in the Talmud, in the Jewish liturgy called the Kaddish, and in certain Jewish morning prayers. So the prayer is really Jesus's summary of important petitions; the words are not new but Jesus intended that they should give a fresh meaning to prayer. The first three requests are for God's glory, the other four refer to human needs.

35

God's nature (v. 9) Matthew uses the phrase 'Our Father in heaven' (literally translated as 'in the heavens'), which emphasizes the spirit of reverence in which God is to be approached. In the Old Testament God is referred to as 'The Father who formed you' (Deuteronomy 32: 6); in Isaiah 63: 16 He is asked to 'look down from heaven, for thou art our Father', which suggests that Matthew may have had that text in mind. Luke simply says 'Father', from the Aramaic word 'Abba', which conveys the warmth and familiarity of a human father.

God's name In the Bible, a person's name was often a clue to his or her character and was sometimes changed to reflect this, for example, 'Jacob', which meant 'cheat', was changed to 'Israel', meaning 'God strives' or 'God rules' (Genesis 32: 22–32). In the Old Testament there are several names used to describe God, such as 'El-Shaddai (God Almighty), Adonai (Master or Lord), 'Elohim (God in the fullness of his power). Jehovah is a later translation of the Hebrew name YHWH, which is never spoken; it is a form of the Hebrew verb 'to be' and means something like 'I am that I am' (Exodus 3: 14).

So God's name, and thus his nature, had been revealed through Jesus and it was to be 'hallowed', from the Greek word 'hagiazo', meaning 'to make sacred'. To hold the name in reverence is to honour the holder of it, which is more positive than merely avoiding using God's name in a profane manner.

God's rule (v. 10) The requests all depend on one another. God's name and nature must be honoured if his Kingdom is to come and his will be done. Matthew uses the phrase 'Kingdom of Heaven' thirty-two times; he is reflecting the Jewish idea expressed in the word 'malkuth', which means 'kingship'. Jesus meant that God's purpose is for people to live in peace and to create a kingdom in which this purpose can be fulfilled. Zechariah 14: 9 puts this point of view emphatically, but the more modern phrase, 'If you want to build a better world, follow the Maker's instructions', offers a more practical interpretation.

'Thy will be done' is not meant to be interpreted as being resigned to accept without complaining whatever injustices life may inflict. It expresses a positive desire and determination to see God's purposes made plain.

Human needs (vv. 11–13)
1. Physical (v. 11)
The word 'daily' is a doubtful one, as far as many manuscripts are concerned, and various suggestions have been made as to its meaning. The Greek word translated as 'daily' occurs only here and in Luke 11: 3. Some scholars prefer 'the day before us', some have 'day by day', while others say it means 'for the morrow' or 'bread just for our existence'. An interesting aside to the debate is that in a household account book from the second century A.D., the word is used to denote 'the day's expenses'.

Some early Christians interpreted this part of the prayer as a plea for enough bread for the daily sacrament, but personally I prefer to regard it as a plea for whatever is necessary to sustain life. This does not mean an expectation to live in luxury, nor does 'give us' mean that we should expect to receive without any effort on our part.

2. Mental (v.12)

To be forgiven for a wrong is most important for real peace of mind. Some translations give the word 'debts' rather than 'trespasses' or 'wrongs' because the Aramaic word for debt, 'hoba', was often used to express the sense that one who had sinned against another was under an obligation to make amends and so 'pay the debt'. Some Christian hymns describe the death of Jesus as 'paying the price of sin'.

Here, however, it does not mean that someone is forgiven by God in proportion to how he has forgiven others or that God's forgiveness can be 'earned' by merit. It means that no one can ask for or expect to receive forgiveness unless he is willing to forgive completely without the reservation 'I'll forgive but not forget'.

3. Moral (v. 13)

The word 'temptation' can mean a test or trial, but God does not 'lead us into temptation' any more than he excuses us from being tested. Being tempted and tested are hazards of everyday life. It is not a sin to find temptation 'crouching at the door', as it did for Cain (Genesis 4: 7), but it is a sin deliberately to open the door and let it in. We cannot always prevent harmful thoughts and feelings coming into our minds, but we can influence how long they stay and what effect they have.

To 'deliver us from evil' is not a request to be protected from risks or rebukes, but a realization that only God *can* rescue us from the sins into which we can so easily slide or be led by others.

So the prayer ends on a note of deliverance, for the words often used at the end – 'For thine is the Kingdom, the power and the glory' – are not in the most reliable manuscripts and were almost certainly added on later for use in church worship. These words are taken from David's prayer in 1 Chronicles 29: 11 and from Psalm 72: 19.

The postscript (vv. 14–15) Once again it is debatable whether this was part of the actual teaching of Jesus or whether it was added on as a commentary to verse 12. However, it is a reminder that forgiveness is a two-way business. Both the one who has sinned and the one who has been wronged have an obligation: for the former must genuinely repent and the latter must do all in his power to bring about a reconciliation.

vv. 16–18 Fasting

Having dealt with the dangers in giving and praying for the wrong reasons, Jesus then talked about fasting, another important aspect of Judaism, although it stemmed more from tradition than from written laws. Many religions see fasting as a desirable means of self-discipline, since a victory in the matter of food can lead to other battles being won in the struggle against self-indulgence of all kinds. In many religions abstinence is advocated as an aid to concentration in meditation.

Jews are expected to fast a few times each year, the most important occasion being Yom Kippur, the Day of Atonement. In addition, in Biblical times, a public fast could be called in the event of catastrophe or crisis, as in the case of Naboth's vineyard (1 Kings 21: 9). In the days of Jesus, however, many Jews fasted twice a week, usually to commemorate the ascent and descent of Mount Sinai by Moses. For some, the 'hypocrites', it had become an occasion to show off their piety.

So Jesus advised his followers to forget the outward signs of fasting – the sad unwashed face, bare feet, ashes on the head, etc. – and to behave as though they were not fasting at all. Such a lack of 'make-up' might mean that the act was not so noticeable, but it would be all the more sincere. Those who used fasting for show had their applause from the public, but God was not impressed unless the motives were genuine.

Part 4

vv. 19–34   Possessions and problems

Having looked at morals and motives, Matthew now turns, in the fourth section of the sermon, to the matter of values. Luke records the same advice but says it was given on a different occasion. The material is usually headed 'Anxiety'; here we shall look at it under two headings.

vv. 19–24   Treasure   (Luke 12: 33–34)

Jesus probably had in mind the practice in those days of putting one's wealth into possessions, rather than keeping it in coinage. People invested in such things as clothes and carpets, pottery and porcelain, and works of art. But such 'treasures' were prone to attacks of all kinds. The word translated as 'rust' literally meant 'eating', suggesting an image of moths eating the fabrics and men breaking through the mud walls to steal the family fortune. The point was that these kinds of treasure were subject to any number of risks, whereas the treasures of truth, love and goodness could be insured against loss through greed and envy.

Does that mean that possessions are wrong?   No, it means that money can be a blessing provided that it is not an end in itself but a means to an end. If a person's whole energies are devoted to gaining possessions or popularity or power, then his 'heart', which is a Jewish image for the centre of life, will be completely absorbed in trying to achieve these things. Even his religion can be turned in this direction. But if the main aim is to further God's Kingdom, then the heart will be absorbed in that and money will be a help towards that end.

The eye test   (vv. 22–23, Luke 11: 34–36)
Of the five senses, eyesight is regarded by many people as the most precious, because with our eyes we make use of the light all around us. It is not surprising, therefore, that the eye in symbolic thought represented enlightenment and moral understanding. A 'good' eye looked for the best and found guidance, but an 'evil' eye denoted a crafty character whose evil acted as a kind of 'cateract' which obscured the light. The Greek word translated here as 'sound' literally meant 'simple, single, uncomplicated', which is essential if the eye is to serve its purpose.

Masters and money   (v. 24, Luke 16:13)   In those days a slave *could* be the property of two people, though it was not very satisfactory or single-minded on the part of the slave. However, the point Jesus made was that someone was mistaken if he imagined that he could give his total allegiance to God's service and still maintain his worship of material things.

'Mammon' is from the Aramaic word 'mamona', which meant 'riches' in a much wider sense than just money. It often indicated a pride in possessions generally. So Jesus was not saying that money itself was evil but that riches can become a rival to religion.

vv. 25–34   Trusting   (Luke 12: 22–32)

The original version of v. 25 – 'Take no thought for your life' – was not very accurate or helpful as it might imply indifference, but the more modern 'be not anxious' is not really strong enough, because Jesus was not talking about provision so much as perspective. He was talking about a sense of values rather than a struggle for survival. He was certainly not advocating an 'opting out', nor was he giving an invitation to idleness.

Food for the birds (v. 26) may be provided, but they will die if they don't do something towards getting it. If people are to make plans for the future they must have a sense of priorities. Solomon in all his royal robes and fine palace might well have thought that those things were the most important, but they were man-made and the little wayside anemones were far more attractive, though their life span was much shorter.

Jesus is not saying, 'don't worry', because worrying is often a matter of temperament. Nor is he talking about things which seem terrible to contemplate but may not happen, and even if they do, may not be as bad as expected, although that advice is implied. He is giving a warning about fretting over things which may seem very important in themselves, but put against the background of greater issues, they will be seen in their true perspective.

It might be said that the remarks about birds and lilies are not really relevant since animals and plants don't have to worry but merely respond to certain instincts. But does that mean that human beings, who have freedom of choice, should be less well looked after by God than the rest of Creation? One thing is certain about anxiety: we can worry ourselves 'to death', but not to a longer life. To put first things first is sound psychology. Most of the 'essentials' which feature in so many publications and advertisements might become less of an obsession if we remember the thousands who die every day because they lack even the basic necessities of life, never mind the luxuries.

To live a day at a time (v. 34) is not easy, but borrowing worries from tomorrow's 'bank' and then spending unnecessary energy and time in their interest is a sure way to drain away our mental reserves. When tomorrow arrives there may be new troubles, but there will also be new strength to face them. As the writer of the Book of Lamentations has it, 'The compassions of the Lord do not fail. They are new every morning.' (3: 23).

It is an interesting exercise to examine what things various people worry most about and to discover whether this is an indication of a person's character.

CHAPTER 7

Part 5

vv. 1–12   True assessments
In what can be seen as Matthew's fifth section of the sermon, he gives Jesus's comments on making criticisms and on making choices.

vv. 1–6   Specks and sawdust   (Luke 6: 37–38, 41–42)
Some have regarded these verses on judgement as guidance to early Christians about taking cases to court. However, it seems much more likely that Jesus was using a humorous analogy, probably from his memories of helping Joseph in the carpenter's shop, to illustrate the danger of condemning faults in others when we are guilty of the same things ourselves.

'Judge not', in the older translations, is not very clear and has led some to think that any kind of judgement or even a critical viewpoint, is forbidden, but Jesus was not saying that at all. He meant that people should be wary of making condemnations that are not just critical but also hypocritical, because they have no right to do so. Concentrating on someone else's faults may reveal the sin of self-righteousness.

The reference to dogs and pigs (v. 6) might be a comment on the 'uncleanness' of certain animals, though it could also be a reference to some early Christian attitudes towards heretics and enemies. Throwing 'pearls to the pigs' indicates how easy it is for something sacred to become desecrated and for something holy to be made profane.

vv. 7–12   Stones and snakes   (Luke 11: 9–13)
Luke puts these verses in a section on prayer, which is possibly their true setting because the point is about being persistent and patient in prayer.

There has to be an active asking and expecting, not just a passive waiting, if the requests are to be rewarded.

The comments on the bread and fish may have been prompted by the proverb about the 'bread of deceit' (Proverbs 20: 17), but since those two things were part of the staple Jewish diet, as seen in the Feeding of the Five Thousand, only a very short-sighted father would have mistaken a flat loaf for a stone, even though the shapes were similar. By referring to things that looked similar but were in fact quite different, Jesus was illustrating the difference between appearance and reality. In addition, his remarks were a reminder of the goodness of God.

It has been pointed out that the words 'asking, seeking, knocking' are on an ascending scale: first we ask, but that is only the beginning, and it must be followed up by a searching and a determined knocking.

Does that mean that God is sometimes reluctant to answer? No, it means that there may be a difference between what we want and what we really need. A father who gives his children whatever they ask for will spoil them and a parent who gives a stone instead of bread will deceive and disappoint them. God does neither of those things. The clue is in v. 11, 'good things to those who ask him'. The essential thing is to ask for what is for our good in the first place. Asking for anything else will not merit much of an answer.

Summing up (v. 12, Luke 6: 31)
This 'golden rule' sums up this section. It is a rule in the sense that it can be applied when there is no time to argue or even to consider the question. It is a ready-made remedy for a situation which needs first-aid rather than complicated surgery.

Jesus was putting into the positive something that had often been noted in the negative. Hillel, a rabbi of the first century B.C., had said, 'What is hateful to you, do not do to your neighbour', and both Confucius and Plato had said very much the same. Today we tend to express it as 'Do as you would be done by'. Whatever the phrasing, it means we should ask ourselves the question how we would want other people – for example, the persecuted, the prisoner, the underprivileged – to treat us if we were in their place.

Isn't even a negative approach better than nothing? It depends on how negative it is. If it means that a person does not harm his neighbour simply through fear of retaliation or if the rule is applied just to keep the peace, then it does not have much merit. But if it means that we do not treat our neighbourhood with anything less than courtesy and respect because we would not want him to treat us with anything less, it becomes a more positive approach. The negative 'I never did him any harm' is not very stimulating, but it is certainly better than the positive doing of evil.

It is interesting to note that Luke uses this verse as an introduction to the demand to love one's enemies, so it is not just a matter of goodwill but a goal to be achieved.

vv. 13–14   The wide gate and the narrow gate   (Luke 13: 24)

Luke uses the idea of a door leading into a house, while Matthew prefers the picture of a gate opening out of the town and leading to a choice between an easy road and a hard road. But the point is the same, namely that because there are plenty of people on a particular road that is no guarantee that they are all going in the right direction. It could be that some are merely taking the line of least resistance and some are going that way simply because everyone else seems to be doing the same.

Real achievement demands a great deal of discipline and dedication, as every Olympic athlete or concert pianist will testify, but once we are through what is often a narrow entrance the effort is worthwhile. It is important to note that Jesus was speaking of entry into real life, rather than mere existence, as both difficult and desirable. He speaks of the gate being 'small' and those who find it 'few', which is different from the ideas of some present-day preachers who tend to make 'being saved' sound very simple.

vv. 15–23   Flocks and fruit   (Luke 6: 43–44, 13: 25–27)

The idea of a 'false' prophet is found frequently in the Old Testament, often as a 'yes man' who will always say what people want him to say or preach what he has been paid to preach. Jeremiah complained bitterly (6: 14) of the prophets who 'cry peace, peace, when there is no peace'. The idea of God's people being 'sheep' was also a popular one (e.g. Psalm 78: 52), while destroyers were sometimes referred to as 'wolves' (Zephaniah 3: 3). Here, false prophets might mean preachers who had crept into the Church under false pretences. But the imposters would be sorted out by their ways rather than by their words.

In an ancient Church writing called the 'Didache', thought to have originated in Syria, the phrase 'false prophets' referred to types of missionaries who were not acceptable to the congregations. People devised all kinds of 'tests' to sort out the genuine prophets from the fakes. For example, if a missionary stayed for more than three days it was seen, for some strange reason, as proof that he was a pretender! Then he was soon sent on his way.

The cry 'Lord, Lord' could be just lip-service, and the casting out of devils was no guarantee of a good relationship with God. Even performing miracles might not indicate a particular power from God, for 'knowing' God (v. 23) meant more than these things.

vv. 24–29   Summary of the sermon

Matthew may have had in mind the way that some of the old Laws concluded by offering the people a choice between 'life or death' (e.g. Deuteronomy 30); the parable of the two builders reflects the same idea.

Perhaps the story was based on an incident Jesus remembered from his youth, when he may have gone with Joseph to inspect a damaged house, or it may have been based on an ancient Jewish proverb which said, 'A man who builds with no good works builds with dry stones, which when the waters come are toppled over'.

Whatever the origin, the point is that firm foundations are essential whether building character or housing. It is futile to talk about a fine structure unless the basic work has been done. Of the four choices that have been mentioned since v. 13 – wide and narrow gates, false and true prophets, good and bad trees and firm or shaky foundations – this last one seems the most obvious. Only a very foolish person would build a house in a place where there was constant danger of collapse, or would imagine that when the storms came they would miraculously miss him. This is the whole point of the sermon. It is intended to give guidance on how to weather the storms of life, not how to avoid them or be excused them.

vv. 28–29   The credentials of Christ   (Mark 1: 22)

To conclude each of the five sections in this gospel, Matthew uses the same formula: 'when Jesus had finished these sayings'. In this instance he uses Mark's summary of Jesus's sermon on the Sabbath at Capernaum. He also refers to the 'crowds' again, after implying at the beginning of the sermon that Jesus was addressing the disciples. He emphasizes their great amazement at the way Jesus taught. The word given as 'amazed' literally meant 'taken out of themselves'. The phrase 'with authority' implied first-hand personal experience and knowledge, as well as complete confidence.

THE SECOND SECTION: CHAPTERS 8,9,10

We saw earlier that Matthew uses a pattern of a nucleus of teaching material being introduced by a suitable theme. In this section the 'mighty works' of 8: 1 – 9 : 34, setting out the kind of 'qualifications' expected of the disciples, especially the need for faith and the ability to heal, lead up to the teaching of 9: 35 – 10: 42 on the subject of the qualities of discipleship. So Matthew begins with some miracles.

The question of miracles

What do we mean by a miracle? Do those found in the Old Testament differ from those found in the New Testament? Did some of them become exaggerated in the telling and, from a mixture of simplemindedness and superstition on the listeners' part, become stories which were swallowed without worrying too much about the ingredients? Were the writers anxious to portray Jesus as a miracle worker because some other religious leaders were said to have the same kind of skill?

Against all that, it must be said that Jesus's powers of healing were acknowledged by his critics, as well as by his supporters. Many who witnessed them, far from thinking it was all a fake, found they had a much deeper sense of awe and wonder. Moreover, when Mark's gospel, which contains many accounts of miracles, appeared there were still plenty of people alive who had witnessed the events and could easily have refuted them if necessary. It is a risky business publishing or broadcasting a survey of a person's life when there are still people who can remember them and, if necessary, reject that particular 'version'.

Of course, many Christians today will admit that some of the miracles in the gospels seem to have a strong psychological element in the cure and that others were symbolic in the sense that they probably had a deeper significance than appeared on the surface. None the less, the spiritual aspect of the miracles cannot be ignored. To me, the real question is not whether Jesus could perform miracles, because if God's nature was within him there is little reason to doubt that, but whether he wanted to be seen merely as a miracle worker; if we take Mark's idea of the 'Messianic secret' seriously, it seems that he did not. In the end, we have to decide how essential the miracles are for a belief that Jesus was the son of God.

However, as far as Matthew is concerned, the healings were evidence that the power of God in Jesus could banish the forces of evil represented by many forms of disease. Following on from the sermon, he now tells of ten miracles, dividing them into three groups. Most of them are copied from Mark, with a little rearranging to suit Matthew's particular purpose, which was to portray Jesus as the model for the Christian missionary.

CHAPTER 8

vv. 1–4   The leper   (Mark 1: 40–45, Luke 5: 12–16)
'Leprosy' was a term applied to different kinds of skin diseases and some translations use the phrase 'dreaded skin disease'. The Greek word 'lepos' meant 'scale'. Contact with a leper was avoided not only for fear of contagion, but in case the 'uncleanness' associated with the disease became attached to the toucher. It was regarded by some as a terrible punishment for sin, so a leper was seen as 'unclean' morally as well as physically. Amongst the many laws in Leviticus 13 and 14 that a leper had to observe was one about 'leaving his hair uncombed, wearing torn clothes and calling out "unclean"', as well as 'living outside the camp, away from others' (Leviticus 13: 46). Today, if treated in its early stages leprosy is curable, but according to the World Health Organization it is becoming more resistant to drugs and seems to be on the increase.

The request   Matthew omits Mark's vivid details, including Jesus's apparent annoyance with the man (the literal translation of Mark 1: 41 is 'anger', not pity), and concentrates on the cure. 'If you will' need not mean that he doubted Jesus's ability or inclination but wondered whether Jesus would actually want to touch him.

The response Jesus quickly bridged the two-metre gap, which was the distance the Law required between a leper and anyone else, and touched the man. He could make him 'clean' but could not 'certify the cure'; that was the prerogative of a priest, who would order the prescribed sacrifice of a 'clean' bird (Leviticus 14: 4–7), so that the man could return to his family.

Why, in a crowd, did Jesus expect secrecy? (v. 4)   Matthew seems to have copied the phrase from Mark without any explanation. Many theories have been suggested concerning this 'secrecy' idea, which is so strong in Mark's gospel. Some say that, because at that stage Jesus did not openly claim to be the Messiah, the secrecy demands were inserted in the gospel to explain why his Messiahship was not widely known. Others suggest that he wanted to avoid being overwhelmed by people who would be interested only in his healing powers, so that he could concentrate on the teaching without any other pressures. In addition, misguided publicity would soon have attracted the attention of the Romans.

vv. 5–13   The sick servant   (Luke 7: 1–10)
Luke has the same story, but though the conversation is the same, the circumstances are different. The material evidently comes from 'Q', but Luke and Matthew interpret it from their particular points of view. Luke wants to show the faith of a foreigner, whereas Matthew, though anxious to include a good word for a gentile, may also be using the incident to describe the dismay of some Jews when they found that at the great 'Messianic banquet', mentioned in certain books of the Apocrypha, there would be more 'outsiders' present than they had anticipated (vv. 11–12).

The centurion He was probably a fairly minor officer in command of a hundred Roman occupation troops, but in matters of faith and concern he was a man of major importance. It is interesting to note that of the centurions mentioned in the gospels and in the Acts of the Apostles only two are named (Acts 10: 1 and 27: 1), but all are written of favourably. The one in this story shows some unusual traits: he cared deeply about his servant (though the Greek word can also mean 'boy' or 'son') and he had remarkable faith in Jesus's ability to heal. Luke also adds that he had built the Jews a synagogue, which made him even more unusual!

The circumstances Luke 'hides' the centurion away, saying that he sent 'some Jewish elders' with his request, but Matthew brings him out into the open. Some readers have seized on Luke's version to disparage the man and to maintain that he did not go in person because he had doubts about whether Jesus would help a foreigner and was afraid that a Jew would have scruples about entering a gentile home. But this does justice to neither him nor Jesus.

It may seem strange that having asked for help, as soon as Jesus agreed, the man didn't want him to come! Perhaps he was overwhelmed by the immediate reaction: in the original Greek the 'I will' is very definite. Perhaps he was expecting some degree of reluctance to help an oppressor and an enemy and felt unworthy at the response to his request. None the less, the main focus is on his amazing faith.

vv. 14–17 The mother-in-law and the 'possessed' (Mark 1: 29–34, Luke 4: 38–41)

Mark says that this happened on a Sabbath and that Peter, James and John were with Jesus. Matthew does not mention the day or the disciples. In his account he emphasizes that just by a touch of the hand Jesus healed Peter's mother-in-law and then just by a word he healed many who were 'possessed by devils'.

In 1 Corinthians 9: 5 Paul indicates that Peter sometimes took his wife with him on preaching journeys, though she is never mentioned in the gospels. Apparently Peter had this time left his wife with her mother whilst he was away with Jesus and he now went back to visit them.

According to Mark, Peter's mother-in-law waited on 'them' when she recovered, but Matthew says 'on him', concentrating his attention on Jesus. Mark indicates that since the first event happened on a Sabbath, after sunset, i.e. when the Sabbath was over, people carried their sick to be healed because work was then permitted. Matthew's attention is absorbed in finding a suitable text to fit the occasion and again he goes to Isaiah, this time to the second Isaiah (the prophet who wrote during the Exile in Babylon) and to one of the 'suffering servant' poems (Isaiah 53: 4), which he changes a little in order to emphasize the healing power of Jesus.

vv. 18–22 What is involved? (Luke 9: 57–62)

Having described three miracles, Matthew diverts for a while, before going on to the second group, to remind would-be followers of the kind of dedication that is needed for real discipleship. Luke refers to three men, Matthew mentions only two.

The impulsive scribe A 'teacher of the law', as they were often known, wanting to be a follower seemed a good 'catch' for the 'fishers of men', for they were often more hostile towards Jesus than helpful, but whether or not the teacher took up the challenge is not clear. He appeared to offer his services unconditionally, but perhaps too hastily, in which case the warning about homelessness may have put him off. Certainly Jesus would not have rejected him because of his background or his beliefs, but to be homeless would have been a daunting prospect.

'Son of Man' (v. 20) could mean a human being, as in Ezekiel 2: 1, or it could mean a kind of heavenly being who would come on the 'clouds of glory' as in Daniel 7: 13; here Jesus seems to be emphasizing his humanity.

Matthew may also be drawing attention to the paradox of the King, having made the earth his home, now being homeless, though earlier he said (4: 13) that Jesus had 'settled at Capernaum'.

The dutiful disciple Burying one's father was an important act and even a priest who would not normally 'render himself unclean for the death of any of his kin' (Leviticus 21: 2–4) was allowed to carry it out. Yet Jesus refused what seemed to be a reasonable request. Why? There are several possible reasons:
1. To carry out that duty would have meant a delay and the demands of the Kingdom couldn't wait.
2. Perhaps Jesus was really saying 'let the spiritually dead tend to one of their own company, you come with me'.
3. If the man's family found out he wanted to follow Jesus, they may well have tried to dissuade him. Indeed, they might have regarded *him* as 'dead'. So Jesus was not being harsh but honest, and Matthew makes the point about counting the cost of discipleship.

8: 23 – 9 : 8   Miracles of power
Matthew now resumes his account of the miracles with another group of three. These illustrate Jesus's power over particularly difficult forces and are presumably intended to show the need for the same kind of decisive approach in his followers.

vv. 23–27   Waves and wonders   (Mark 4: 35–41, Luke 8: 22–25)
A number of 'explanations' have been suggested for this miracle, including one based on the geographical fact that the Lake of Galilee is at the northern end of the ravine known as the Great Rift Valley and is some 180 metres below sea-level. The air can move very quickly down this 'tunnel' and storms often start and end abruptly. (This and other points are discussed more fully in the commentary on Mark's gospel.) But that explanation is far from satisfactory and portrays both the disciples and Jesus in a very poor light. Moreover it is difficult to believe that the experienced seamen amongst the disciples would have been deceived by such events.

It is important to bear in mind how much Old Testament influence is at work in this story. For example, the ability to control tempests was regarded as a sign of divine power (Psalm 89: 8) and the image of 'the deep' was used to describe evil forces from which God could save those with faith (Psalm 18: 16, and most explicitly Psalm 107: 29, 'When in distress I cried to the Lord, the storm sank to a murmur and the waves of the sea were stilled'). Add to that the idea that to sleep peacefully was a sign of complete trust in God (Psalm 4: 8) and we have a background against which this story is more easily understood.

Whatever the actual details, the symbolism would have been clear to early Christians. Jesus was asleep, in complete faith and trust, which the disciples mistook for indifference. When he awoke and quietened the storm he also quietened the panic in the disciples themselves and they realized that they were in the presence of someone who could cope with problems which they couldn't face. Matthew misses out some of Mark's details, including the words 'Hush! Be still!', but the word he uses to describe the storm, 'seismos', meaning 'violent shaking', shows the fury and the force of the waves. It wasn't an ordinary storm and it was not an ordinary experience.

v. 28-34   Tombs and torments   (Mark 5: 1–20,   Luke 8: 26–39)

Matthew gives fewer details of this story than Mark does, but he compensates for that by saying there were two men instead of one!

Why does he 'double up' like this?
It is not at all clear but several suggestions have been made:
1. It was a kind of 'editorial habit' that Matthew had. He does the same thing in 9: 27 and 20: 30.
2. He uses exaggeration to increase the dramatic impact.
3. He thought that a 'legion of devils' (Mark 5: 9), which could be as many as 6000, was too much to be in one man!
4. It is a combination of two stories, both about possession by evil spirits.
5. Matthew is right – there *were* two men – and Mark and Luke were both wrong.

The place   Matthew has 'Gadarenes', but Gadara was several miles from the lake. Mark's 'Gerasenes' is equally unlikely because Gerasa is also too far away. So Luke's 'Gergesenes' is probably the correct place, since the sites of Kersa and Gerge are found on the eastern shore of the lake today. Josephus, perhaps because of the apparent confusion, calls the whole district 'Gadaritis'.

The person   Whether singular or plural, the man or men were definitely 'possessed' by demons, if we accept that particular analysis of mental illness. Evil powers were believed to be of different kinds and were thought to take the form of 'unclean spirits' capable of entering the bodies and minds of people and animals, causing all kinds of chaos and illness. Matthew does not give any names, nor does he mention the number of pigs. He does not even make it clear whether the madmen were cured and whether they wanted to follow Jesus afterwards, as Mark indicates. Matthew's purpose seems to be to focus on the fact that although the evil spirits were formidable (v. 28) they met their match in Jesus.

The problem   Some scholars are rather sceptical of this story, regarding it as just a folk story which circulated amongst somewhat simple people in 'pagan' territory. Some believe that the story of the pigs falling into the lake was once completely separate from the story of the madman, but that the two later became combined and confused. Others see a significance in the fact that this is a gentile area and that it was into 'unclean' animals that the demons were driven. So, they argue, the territory was 'cleansed' by Jesus and thus prepared for later preaching, a task, they point out, that Mark says the man was told to go and do.

If we wonder why there are so many 'interpretations', it must be borne in mind that such a story as this would have passed through various stages in its telling before it reached the form in which we now have it, and if each stage added another aspect it is not surprising that in its final form in the gospels it contains variations which prompt different explanations. To suggest that Jesus *caused* the pigs to be drowned is unlikely. He may have used something that was already happening to convince the 'possessed' man, in the only way he could understand, that the 'spirits' had left him.

The parting   The outcome of it all was that the local inhabitants did not revile Jesus, they just requested him to leave. They made their choice and he did not try to dissuade them. He had cured a madman, but in the process had disturbed their lives and their livelihood which, according to Mark, made them 'afraid', and made Jesus no longer acceptable. Even if we take the story as more of a parable than a miracle, as some do, that point is important.

CHAPTER 9

vv. 1–8   Faithful friends   (Mark 2: 1–12, Luke 5: 17–26)

Mark and Luke give more details about this story, telling how the four men, unable to get into the house and determined to get their paralysed friend to Jesus, made a hole in the roof and lowered him down. Matthew does not mention this, simply saying that the man was brought to Jesus. He seems to prefer to concentrate on the authority displayed by Jesus in effecting the cure.

The criticism   This was a result of Jesus's claim to forgive sins. Jews were used to thinking of sins being forgiven 'in the name of God' because only God had the authority to forgive sins, but for a man to claim to do so by his own authority would be regarded as blasphemy. It should be noted, however, that the word usually meant 'cursing against God'. The lawyers did not openly criticize him, but Jesus seemed to know what they were thinking.

The cure   The friends or relatives had carried the man but they could not cure him. Jesus knew that before the man could be cured he had to be convinced that his condition was not the result of sin. So Jesus told him to take courage because his sins – real or imagined – were forgiven, so he could forget the idea that his sickness was caused by sin. The man's sense of guilt disappeared and already the cure had started. *Then* Jesus told him to get up and walk, showing that he had authority not only to forgive sins but also to heal.

Did Jesus perform this miracle for the man's sake or to confound his critics? It is one of the few miracles where Jesus took the initiative and spoke first, before being approached or appealed to, and at first sight it seems that but for the implied criticism about blasphemy, Jesus might not have performed the miracle at all. But surely if the point of this incident had been to confound his critics, then the gospels would have shown that the scribes were convinced by the evidence; however, there is no indication that they were or that they took any further interest in the incident. So it seems that the miracle was inspired by the faith of the man's friends.

vv. 9–13   Tax-collectors and outcasts   (Mark 2: 13–17, Luke 5: 27–32)

The person   All the synoptic gospels agree that Jesus invited a tax-collector to be a disciple, but they do not agree about his identity. He was almost certainly a customs official at Capernaum, collecting taxes at a roadside booth on goods taken out of the town.

Our modern idea of a tax official gives little idea of a tax-collector in those days. He was not, as a rule, paid a salary; instead he worked on a commission basis. Every region was assessed by the Romans for taxation purposes and they often sold the right to collect the money to the highest bidder. He would then 'rent out' the area to lesser officials who would pay him for the privilege, so this second group – to which Matthew may well have belonged – had to make enough money to pay their superior and to make their own living. The occupation was therefore open to all kinds of corruption and extortion, which made people despise the tax-collectors. The fact that they worked for a foreign power increased the contempt further.

Tax-collecting was an occupation that may have provided good money but did not confer much respect. Indeed, a tax-collector's standing in society was so low that his evidence was not acceptable in a court of law and he was always associated with 'sinners'. The older versions of the gospels describe them as 'publicans' from the Latin 'publicani', which referred to the Roman collectors of revenue.

Mark names the tax-collector as 'Levi, son of Alphaeus', yet in his full list of disciples (3: 14) Levi is not mentioned, but Matthew is, with James being described as the 'son of Alphaeus'. Luke follows Mark in this. Matthew, however, says that the tax-collector at Capernaum was called 'Matthew' and in his full list of disciples (10: 3) repeats the name and the occupation.

Various suggestions have been made to explain this discrepancy:
1. Matthew and Levi were the same person, who had two names, though to have two Jewish names would be unusual.
2. James and Matthew were both sons of Alphaeus.
3. The phrase 'tax-collector' in Matthew 10: 3 originally referred to James, whose name is next, but a copier thought it referred to Matthew.

The pettiness   Whatever the name, Jesus's choice of such a person for a disciple caused considerable consternation. The Pharisees did not criticize him for caring about an outcast, but when he accepted an invitation to eat with such 'sinners' they were outraged because to eat with a person was a sign not only of friendship, but of having a common interest.

The 'patients'   The house where the meal took place suddenly became a consulting room when the 'doctor' diagnosed the needs of his 'patients'. A person does not usually consult a doctor unless there is need and an acknowledgement of illness. It would be strange, too, for a doctor to associate only with the healthy, for then he would not be doing his job. Jesus may have had a well-known proverb in mind – said to come from the Greek philosopher, Diogenes – 'A physician does not practise his profession amongst those who are well.'

The prescription, according to Matthew, was to go and study the words of Hosea 6: 6, though the quotation is perhaps not the most fitting in these circumstances.

vv. 14–17   Old forms, new fashions   (Mark 2: 18–22, Luke 5: 33–39)

The synoptic writers do not seem very sure who asked this question on fasting, which started the comments on coats and patches. Mark says it was 'some people', Luke simply says 'they', whilst Matthew says it was some disciples of John the Baptist. The latter are not mentioned much in the synoptic accounts, but they may have played a larger part in the stories than we realize.

The question   It concerned fasting, possibly referring to voluntary fasting rather than the obligatory fasting expected on certain occasions. It seems that John's disciples fasted more often than the Law demanded, which was perhaps commendable but not, according to Jesus, really in keeping with the ideas of the Kingdom. They could not understand why Jesus's disciples did not at least join in occasionally.

The answer   Jesus used an analogy about a wedding, something that often went on for several days. At such an occasion, when food was one of the first considerations, fasting was probably the last thing that would be considered! In Judaea, even students of the Torah were allowed to leave their studies for such an occasion. So Jesus's coming and his good news about God were reasons for celebration, not sadness. There would be a time for fasting when he was 'taken away' from them.

Garments and goatskins (vv. 16–17)   These two short parables make the same point. If people wanted to keep their old ways – the old 'coats and containers' of religion – then they could continue to use the old materials; there would be no pressure and no problems. But if new ideas and concepts of religion were to be adopted, they would need new forms. To people who were poor, the idea of 'making do' with old clothes or wineskins was always appealing but not always practical.

The word 'tear' in v. 16 comes from the Greek 'skhisma'; from this we get 'schism', describing a split in the Church.

The Greek word for 'fresh' (v. 17) literally means 'of a new kind', not seen before.

vv. 18-34 Faith and a funeral

Matthew now gives a third group of miracles. There are four, all copied from Mark, but 'edited' by Matthew.

vv. 18–26 Disease and death (Mark 5: 21–43, Luke 8: 40–56)

Mark cleverly combines the two stories of Jairus's daughter and the woman with haemorrhages, giving plenty of drama and detail, but Matthew omits these 'extras' and just gives the bare essentials to show the faith and the cure.

The man: Matthew does not mention his name but uses the word 'archon' to describe him, which could be applied to various officials of the synagogue who were able to preside over the services. The translation varies between 'ruler' and 'president', or just 'official'.

The message According to Matthew, the daughter had just died, whereas Mark says she was 'at death's door'. Matthew seems to want to show the man's faith in believing that Jesus could raise the dead, even though such a miracle has not so far been recorded in this gospel. He also says that the disciples went with Jesus, but omits any mention of the crowds who, according to Mark, were hemming Jesus in on all sides (Mark 5: 24).

The faith (v. 20) The woman's illness, whatever it was, had not responded to treatment: according to Mark, she had spent all her money on consulting doctors but they had not helped her in the least. Her illness made her 'unclean' (Leviticus 15: 25) which is probably why she wanted to touch Jesus from behind, to avoid being seen, and to touch only his clothes so that she would not 'contaminate' him by her touch. But one thing that was not hidden was her faith in Jesus.

The fringe (v. 21) This was the 'tzitzith' or tassel of the robe, which hung over the left shoulder and reached almost to the ground. It was the sacred part because into it was often woven a violet or blue thread and whenever this thread was seen 'You will remember all my [God's] commands and obey them' (Numbers 15: 39). Perhaps the woman touched the hem of Jesus's robe with this idea in mind, but it is more likely that she just thought she could become well without anyone, including Jesus, being any the wiser.

Matthew omits the vital verse that Jesus was *aware* that power had gone from him. Perhaps this is because the idea of 'power' ('dunamis') being

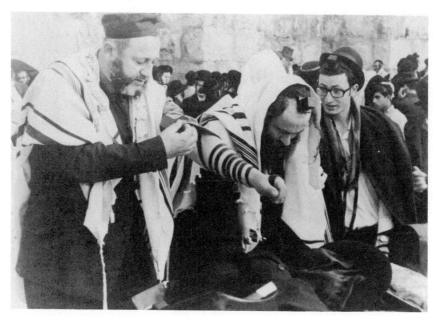

Jews wearing talliths (prayer shawls) and tefillin in modern Israel

transmitted from one person to another was a feature of pagan worship and Matthew wanted to avoid any suspicion of superstition or 'mind over matter'. He also omits the 'fear and trembling' on the woman's part.

The funeral (vv. 23–26)   Professional mourners were often hired to weep at funerals; even very poor people would have at least 'two flute players and a wailing woman'. At Jairus's home, since he was probably quite wealthy, there seemed to be a number of these mourners already at work, but Jesus ordered them all out, telling them that they were a bit premature.

Was the daughter really dead?   It is sometimes suggested that she was only in a coma and that the words of Jesus should be taken literally (v. 24). But 'sleep' was a euphemism often used for death and the Greek word here is the same as that used by Paul (Ephesians 5: 14), 'Awake, sleeper, rise from the dead', implying that sleep was death but that there would be an awakening. To all appearances the girl was certainly dead, but it must be remembered that in those days medical knowledge was limited and they could have been mistaken.

vv. 27–31 'Double vision'
This seems to be Matthew's version of Mark's miracle at Bethsaida (Mark 8: 22–26), but with the 'two-in-one' treatment again, although if it is copied from Mark it has been changed considerably. Matthew is vague about the

location, but not about the result – or about the request for secrecy. It is similar to the warning given to the leper in Mark 1: 43.

vv. 32–34   Deaf and dumb
This is a little like the story in Mark 7: 32, but more similar to the one in Luke 11: 14, which suggests that it might have come from 'Q'. This time Matthew does not double the number of men, but he does give a very similar story in 12: 22. The word used here could mean deaf as well as dumb, as the two afflictions are often combined.

There are no details of how the cure was effected, instead the emphasis is on the amazement of the onlookers and the Pharisees' suggestion that Jesus's power to drive out demons resulted from him being in league with the chief of demons. This is something that Matthew deals with more fully in Chapter 12.

vv. 35–38   Preaching and pity
This short section is not only a glimpse of a mission of which we know very little and an illustration of how incomplete the gospels are. It is also an example of Matthew taking a few 'fragments' from other gospels, especially the remarks about the harvest from Luke 10: 2, and using them as an introduction to Jesus's teaching. This is the beginning of a section of teaching which continues in Chapter 10.

CHAPTER 10   INSTRUCTIONS TO THE TWELVE

The ten miracles which Matthew has just related are part of his plan in this section to show the way in which a follower of Christ should work. That is why he focused on the essential elements in the stories, such as the faith and the power to heal. Now, in the nucleus of his 'second book', he concentrates on the choosing and commissioning of the disciples and the warnings about what they will face in the future. As in the Sermon on the Mount, he selects material from different sources and puts it together to form a kind of 'working manual'.

v. 1–4   Choosing the Twelve   (Mark 3: 13-19, Luke 6: 12–16)
According to Mark, the Twelve were selected early on when Jesus was just beginning his work. Matthew has left it until later, to show that the Twelve were the 'spearhead' of the movement and key men in the Kingdom. Twelve tribes represented Israel, now twelve men would represent the *new* Israel.

Did they do so?   Not if we take the gospels as the whole story, because it soon becomes obvious that though some of the disciples were prominent in many of the stories, others are conspicuous only by their absence. In fact, after this 'introduction' little or nothing is known of the majority of them, except from tradition and legend. Matthew uses the words 'disciple' and 'apostle' to describe them. Disciple means 'student' or 'learner', and apostle means 'messenger' or someone who represents a person of authority, so Matthew was using both words to convey the double role of the Twelve.

Why do we know so little about some of them? That is a mystery to which all kinds of solutions have been suggested, but none seems to be satisfactory. It may be that the only stories which have survived are those involving the disciples who later become leaders in the Church, especially Peter, or perhaps some of them were not so prominent because they were not so popular or they were more self-effacing. Perhaps some had other responsibilities which meant they were not always present, they may even have taken it in turns to travel around with Jesus, rather than all being with him all the time. The main point is that he managed to 'mould' them together to work as a team, although in many ways they were so different.

The names A list of the disciples is given four times in the New Testament – in the synoptic gospels and in the Acts of the Apostles (1: 13) – but there are differences in some of the names. John's gospel mentions a man (Nathanael) apparently not named in the synoptics and a second-century document called 'Epistle to the Apostles' includes a list that is different again. So where does this leave us in trying to identify them?

Some suggestions:

Simon is named first in the lists. To his Jewish name 'Simeon' is added the Greek 'Petros', meaning 'rock' or 'stone', from which we get 'Peter'. The Aramaic 'Kephas' had the same meaning. Perhaps his additional name indicated the kind of character Jesus hoped Simon would develop.

Andrew was Simon's brother, but is rarely mentioned with the 'favoured three', Peter, James and John. According to John's gospel (1: 40), he was John the Baptist's disciple before he followed Jesus. Tradition has it that he was crucified at Patras in Achaia on a cross shaped like the letter X. (This is why it is known at St Andrew's Cross.) Since the eighth century he has been the patron saint of Scotland.

James and John are often 'on the stage' but very rarely speak. Their father, Zebedee, was a fisherman and their mother, according to Matthew 27: 56, was one of the women at the cross. Matthew omits Mark's reference to the name 'Boanerges', perhaps because he did not think of them as 'sons of thunder' or because he wondered whether that was the word's true meaning. There is a theory that the word could be connected with the idea of 'twins' or 'pairs'.

Philip, like Andrew, was also a Greek name. Philip's home was in Bethsaida (John 1: 44). After this, he is mentioned again only in John's gospel.

Bartholomew may have been a 'patronymic', a name derived from the father's name. 'Bar' means 'son of', so he may have been the son of 'Tolmai'. Some think he is the 'Nathanael' of John 1: 45.

Thomas is another one who appears again only in John's gospel. There he is portrayed as a sceptic when he at first doubted the resurrection of Jesus (John 20: 25), thus he is often known as 'Doubting Thomas', though his nickname in that gospel is 'Didymus' which means 'twin'. According to tradition, Thomas became a missionary in India and today a place near Madras is known as 'St Thomas's Mount'.

Matthew   This name appears in all the lists, but his identity is uncertain.

James, son of Alphaeus is mentioned in all the lists, but very little is known of him, unless he is 'James the Less', which may indicate his rank, or even his height!

Lebbaeus   Some manuscripts have 'Thaddaeus' and one reads 'Lebbaeus, whose surname was Thaddaeus'. (Perhaps the scribe was trying to solve the difficulty of two names!) Luke has 'Judas, the son of James' instead, perhaps the 'other Judas' in John 14: 22.

Simon was sometimes called the 'Canaanite' from the Hebrew 'Kana', which meant 'zealous', indicating that he was a member of the Zealot or Zelote political party in Galilee, a fanatical guerrilla movement started by Judas the Galilean at the beginning of the first century and pledged to fight the Roman conquerors.

Judas 'Iscariot' is often taken to mean 'man of Kerioth', a town in southern Judaea. Another interpretation is that it came from the Latin 'sicarius', meaning 'assassin'. Some scholars associate the name with the Aramaic 'ishkaraya', which meant 'false'. John's gospel simply says that he was the son of Simon Iscariot (13: 2).

Why is there such confusion about the names?   With such an important group of people, it would be expected that the writers would have got the names right. But perhaps that is part of the problem: the disciples may have been so well known that different names were used and everyone then, if not now, would have known which one was meant. Another possibility is that they may have had several names, or even a Jewish name and a Greek name.

vv. 5–42   Instructions and advice
Now that the 'troops' were assembled, Matthew tells of their 'marching orders' for their mission and the warnings about the problems they will face.

vv. 5–15   'Start among your own people'   (Mark 6: 7–13, Luke 9: 1–6)
Some scholars wonder whether Jesus really advised the disciples to avoid Samaritan towns, but perhaps it was meant purely as practical guidance. Missionary work, like charity, can begin at home and many Jews – the 'lost

sheep of Israel' – needed reminding of the Kingdom of Heaven just as much as Samaritans did.

They were to carry no money – though it is doubtful whether they would have had much 'gold and silver' to take – and no 'extras' and should earn any hospitality they might receive. They were to go in peace and if there was a peaceful response, a blessing would rest upon the home, but if not the wish would return to the giver and would be given to someone else. The reason for these restrictions was that they should not expect any reward or give way to any kind of greed. God would provide and they must trust him, though presumably the 'worthy people' (v. 11) would be the sort who would be sympathetic towards the mission.

Shaking the dust off their feet (v. 14) was something that some of the more extreme Jews would do before returning to Jewish territory. Here, however, it is probably meant to indicate a retreat in the face of indifference. Such an attitude had been encountered in Sodom (Genesis 19), where there had been terrible ill-treatment of visitors.

vv. 16–25 Sheep and serpents (Mark 13: 9–13, Luke 21: 12–17)

Some believe that this section is a later addition to the instructions about local journeys because it deals with wider dangers and difficulties, such as the followers later faced when the Christians were persecuted by enemies and heretics. However, the main point is not the potential persecution or punishments, but the promise of help that would be given by the Holy Spirit to face them. History has seen some terrible persecution of people for all kinds of reasons, but it has also seen many examples of men and women who have refused to be overwhelmed or defeated by disaster.

Beelzebub (v. 25) The word came from 'Baal-zebub', the Philistine God of Ekron (2 Kings 1: 2). By a play on words – putting in the Hebrew 'zebel', which meant 'manure' – the word could become 'Baalzebul' or 'Beelzebul', meaning 'Lord of the Flies', instead of its original 'Lord of the Mansion'. In the gospels it was meant to denote 'Lord of the Demons'.

vv. 26–39 Secrets and sparrows (Luke 12: 2–9, 51–53, 14: 26–27)

A rabbi would sometimes speak very quietly to his disciples because he did not wish his whispering to be 'broadcast'. By contrast, public announcements were often shouted from the housetops or roofs of synagogues. Here, Jesus was encouraging the disciples to publish the good news as much as possible.

The 'soul-destroyer' (v. 28) sounds very sombre; it almost certainly refers to God himself. Although Satan could lead someone into evil, only God could destroy the 'soul'.

What is 'the soul'?
The word had two main meanings:
1. The 'life principle' of living animals and beings. The Greek word is

'psyche' and it includes emotions and understanding, but is something that ceases to exist at death.

2. The human reason and personality: the 'pneuma'. This is the 'spirit' which God gives to the body, but which differs from the body and is not destroyed by death.

Here the word seems to mean 'self'.

vv. 29–31 Bird-watching!

In the Old Testament the word 'sparrow' could be a general term for small birds, but the Greek word used here referred to the common sparrow which was sometimes caught and sold as food to poor people. The price was probably much less than 'two for a penny', or a 'denarius', a silver coin equivalent to a day's wage for a labourer. Jesus was comparing the price of a sparrow and the number of hairs with the greatness of God's providence.

vv. 32–36 Costs and contrasts

Matthew is still pursuing the theme of persecution. Even when the confession of belief in Christ may be very costly, the follower must still be faithful.

'The sword' (v. 34) has often caused controversy as to its meaning. Certainly, some Christians later knew what it meant for such a weapon to be used against them, but to 'bring' a sword and to set one person against another is a serious matter. Luke's version has 'to set fire' and 'to bring division', which is almost the same.

It cannot be the *purpose* of Christ to bring conflict, but the Christian faith *has* brought divisions, sometimes, sadly, because of narrowness and biogtry, but sometimes because Christians showed a determination to do what they believed to be right whatever the cost or consequence. Many people have found that to attempt to put the Christian gospel into practice invites antagonism and opposition. To be neutral in the struggle between good and evil may be weakness, to take sides may cause division.

vv. 37–39 The cross and commitment

Again, it has been questioned whether Jesus actually said some of these words, though Matthew's 'love less' is a more acceptable phrase than Luke's 'hate'. Jesus was not advocating an active dislike of parents, he was saying that a follower must care for him even more than for the family, dear as they may be. Many people have had to make this choice: for example, when St Francis of Assisi decided to be a monk rather than a merchant like his father, his family disowned him. This kind of decision can be a 'cross' that someone has to take up.

vv. 40–42 Conclusion of second section (Mark 9: 41)

Matthew concludes with a reminder that real discipleship is much more

58

than preaching or prophesying. It is the ability to welcome the ones who come in God's name and to give sustenance to the weak, which is what 'little ones' really means. A cup of cold water was not insignificant, it could often mean considerable sacrifice, not only because water was precious but also because getting it might have entailed a long walk to the well.

Chapter 11 verse 1 is the usual formula for the end of a discourse.

Did the disciples go out and follow these instructions? In his gospel Matthew makes no mention of them doing so, though the Acts of the Apostles gives plenty of evidence that they did. From the study of ancient church writings called the 'Didache' or 'The teachings of the Twelve Apostles', discovered in 1883, it is evident that there were many missionaries in the early Church, composed of 'teachers, prophets and apostles'. Perhaps Matthew had these people in mind in his second section.

THE THIRD SECTION: 11: 2 – 13: 52

This section is centred on the teaching by parables, in Chapter 13, about the Kingdom of Heaven. It is addressed to the crowds, rather than to the disciples, and is really an apologetic, or defence, of the Christian faith against its critics. Matthew describes an increasing tendency on some people's part to doubt Jesus and to oppose him, and he is determined to defend Jesus's claims to be the true 'Deliverer'. So he divides this third section into two main parts, the questions raised and the answers given. He spells out the doubts and fears, then gives some assurances to allay the fears.

CHAPTER 11

vv. 2–11 The plea from prison (Luke 7: 18–35)

If Matthew wanted to show that some people had begun to wonder whether or not Jesus really was the Messiah, who better to start with than the man who had seemed so sure of it? Of all the people who had appeared ready to accept Jesus, John the Baptist had seemed the most fervent, yet here he is sending two of his disciples to ask whether Jesus really was the one they wanted. Matthew is so anxious to ask this question that he forgets to tell us *why* John was in prison, though he does so later.

The prison: According to Josephus (*Antiquities* XVIII 5: 2) it was the fortress of Machaerus, on the shores of the Dead Sea.

The purpose Perhaps there is more in the question than meets the eye. Did the question originate from John or were his disciples a little resentful of the fact that *their* leader was in prison, whilst the one to whom he had deferred was still out preaching. It is possible that their visit had a little to do with rivalry as well as with research. This seems to be reflected in their question

(v. 3), which is similar to a phrase found in the writings of the Mandaeans, a sect which regarded John as the Messiah.

But whatever lay behind it, the question remained: was Jesus the true Messiah or not? If not, they would look elsewhere.

Why the doubts? Probably John had heard reports about Jesus which did not, in his mind, add up to the Jewish image of the Messiah. He had no doubt heard of Jesus breaking the Sabbath rules, associating with 'sinners' and criticizing the Commandments. He was apparently *not* wielding the 'axe of judgement' or 'sorting out the wheat from the chaff', and the 'fires of judgement' seemed to be a bit slow in starting! This made John uncertain.

The promise Jesus's answer was to defend the one who had doubted him, though some see in the words a rebuke. He told the messengers to report the wonders they had witnessed – all things expected of a Messiah (e.g. Isaiah 35: 5) – and then let John decide for himself. Perhaps the reference to the blind and deaf was a little ironic, bearing in mind John's apparent 'blindness'.

The 'stumbling-block' (v. 6) is a strong expression. It literally means 'to cause someone to lose faith' so Jesus was warning against the dangers of finding fault without knowing the full facts.

The praise Whether or not John was convinced is not told, but when the messengers had gone Jesus paid him a great tribute, first by saying what he *was not* – a wavering reed – and then what he *was* – a powerful prophet and the fulfilment of Malachi 3: 1. He was 'greater than any mother's son', which was a remarkable testimony to the way he had carried out the work he had been given to do, yet he was prepared to be 'the least' in the Kingdom, as far as privilege and position were concerned. Verse 11 is the only place in Matthew's gospel where the title 'John the Baptist' is used.

vv. 12–19 The indecision

Matthew has drawn attention to John's doubts and now he shows the hesitancy of the people by means of reference to a children's game in which the children argued about whether they were doing a dance or a dirge. John's Nazirite way of life was too austere, Jesus's 'liberal' attitude was too lax. So what kind of Messiah *did* they want?

vv. 20–24 The indifference (Luke 10: 13–15)

Following the remarks about the crowd, Matthew goes on to deal with the apathy of whole towns. Very little is known about some of them, apart from the fact that they were apparently noted for their refusal to repent of their ways.

Bethsaida is mentioned very rarely in the gospels, though Mark says that a blind man was healed there (Mark 8: 22). The name meant 'house of fishing'. Herod Philip called it Bethsaida Julius in honour of the daughter of the Emperor Augustus.

Chorazin may be the present ruin known as Karaze to the north-west of Tell Hum (believed to be the site of Capernaum) because the fourth-century writer Eusebius said it was only two Roman miles from Capernaum.

Capernaum was the centre of Jesus's Galilean ministry, so why was it singled out for such criticism? Perhaps its commerce and prosperity were causing complacency. The words bear a striking resemblance to Isaiah's criticism of the King of Babylon (Isaiah 14: 15).

Tyre and Sidon were denounced by Amos and the writers of the Books of Kings for their wealth and wickedness. They were also condemned for such crimes as ill treating prisoners and producing Jezebel! Towns exist on the same sites today.

Sodom was notorious for its vices and violence both at the beginning and at the end of the Bible (Genesis 18 and Revelation 1: 8). It was known as the 'city of sin'. The towns that had heard Jesus preach would suffer a worse fate even than such places as Sodom because they had less excuse for continuing in their evil ways.

vv. 25–30 The invitation (Luke 10: 21–22)

These verses are sometimes called the 'Ecstasy' of Jesus and are in striking contrast to the previous verses. It is a burst of confidence and supreme consciousness of a oneness with God that blazes like a torch from the darkness which Matthew is describing. Perhaps he wants to show that despite all the doubts about Jesus from the 'wise', the simple, ordinary people accepted him.

This is followed by the great invitation to all who were burdened, not only in body, but in mind, to come to Christ and find true rest and peace of mind. He was not offering release from the 'yoke', because life always has responsibilities and cares, but he offered a different kind of yoke, one which faith and hope made lighter. In those days a yoke, used to hold two working animals together, could be a light wooden one or a heavy iron one. The second type was harsh and heavy and often referred to symbolically to describe slavery under a foreign power or a harsh ruler (e.g. 1 Kings 12: 4). Again, like the plank and sawdust (7: 1–5) this may have been a memory from Jesus's carpenter's-shop days.

What did he mean by 'gentle and humble'? (v. 29) It did not mean being afraid to speak out against evil. The hymn which begins 'Gentle Jesus meek and mild' has often given the wrong impression, though Charles Wesley (its author) would have not wished it to. One of the essential elements of greatness is gentleness when dealing with people who are in need and Jesus's gentleness and courtesy were always evident, though his actions against evil were strong and effective.

CHAPTER 12

vv. 1–14   Two examples of a 'lighter yoke'

Matthew now goes on to give two examples of how the burden of trying to keep the Sabbath Laws could be lightened by a more enlightened attitude. He also wants to show that Jesus was 'sovereign' even over the Sabbath.

Why is the Sabbath so special to Jews?   There are many reasons, but it is principally because in the first Creation story (Genesis 1) God rested on the seventh day, so the day became a 'Shabbat', or 'rest' day. In addition, the fourth commandment decreed that the day must be kept 'holy', which meant there should be no work. After the experience of slavery in Egypt, the Jews regarded it as important to have a day of rest, so no work was permitted on the Sabbath. Later, after the return from the Exile in Babylon, the importance of the Sabbath was stressed again, especially by Nehemiah and Ezekiel. In the days of Jesus, the Sabbath had become one of the most safeguarded of all the Jewish institutions, though there was much debate about what exactly constituted 'work'.

vv. 1–8   The cornfield controversy   (Mark 2: 23–28, Luke 6: 1–5)

The deed   Why the Pharisees were there is not stated, but their criticism of the disciples was clear. According to Deuteronomy 23: 24, to pick corn in another man's field was allowed, so the disciples were not being accused of stealing. However, to pick corn on a Sabbath was 'reaping' and to rub the grains in the hands was 'threshing', so that was regarded as working on the Sabbath.

The defence   Since the Pharisees had referred to the Old Testament for their 'prosecution' of the disciples, Jesus did the same for their defence. It is interesting to note that Matthew does not copy Mark's mistake about the High Priest. Probably he realized that Mark meant Ahimelech, not Abiathar (1 Samuel 21: 2), but rather than correct him, he omitted any reference to the man.

In v. 5 Matthew refers to an exception allowed by the rabbis themselves, based on Numbers 28: 9–10, and then includes a prophecy from Hosea (6: 6) about mercy. The point was that human need is more important than religious rules and, moreover, the action did not in any way violate the spirit of the Sabbath, which was the holiness of the day.

vv. 9–14   The synagogue scandal   (Mark 3: 1–6, Luke 6: 6–11)

The scene changes to the synagogue, where the paralysed-arm incident seems suspiciously like a pre-arranged plot to try to trick Jesus. Healing was allowed on the Sabbath if it was thought that life was in danger, but this man's condition was not critical, because it could wait until the Sabbath was over, without getting worse, so to heal him would be work which should have been avoided.

Luke says that it was the man's right hand that was paralysed, but Matthew is not specific. He also leaves out Mark's report of Jesus's question about taking or saving life on the Sabbath, presumably because he thinks that it might 'sidetrack' the main issue. Instead he includes the statement about a man being more important than a sheep. Matthew does not include Mark's reference to the Herodians, mentioning only the Pharisees.

Jesus's point was that 'doing good' (v. 12) should surely include helping a man with a handicap, and not just visiting the sick.

vv. 15–21   The suffering servant

Aware of the hostility, Jesus went away and worked elsewhere, though Matthew does not say where he went to. Matthew's intention is to emphasize that whatever the opposition might believe, Jesus was the true servant of God and, as usual, a prophecy is given to prove it.

The prophecy is from the second Isaiah (42: 1–3), a writer who was with the Jews during the Exile in Babylon (586–539 B.C.) and who was the author of Chapters 40–55 of the book bearing the name 'Isaiah'. Judaism believes that this Isaiah did not refer to the Messiah, but Christianity interprets the 'suffering servant' theme as referring to the Messiah, though this image differs greatly from that of other Old Testament writers. The second Isaiah says that the Messiah would be a 'suffering servant', a difficult concept to understand, but meaning that victory would come through vicarious suffering, i.e. bearing the suffering for other people's sins.

Isaiah described the 'Servant of the Lord' in four poems, of which this quotation is the first, though Matthew has adapted it slightly to suit his purpose of showing Jesus as the real representative of God and as the proclaimer of 'justice to the Gentiles'. It could be said that Matthew's version is more a reflection upon rather than a reproduction of Isaiah's words.

vv. 22–37   Continuing controversy   (Mark 3: 20–30, Luke 11: 14–23)

Matthew now returns to the criticisms, this time introduced by the arguments about the healing of the blind and dumb man. He uses Mark's story but carefully avoids any reference to Jesus being 'out of his mind', given in Mark. He wants to avoid any suggestion of 'possession', in an age when the idea that certain people were motivated by the power of demons was widespread. To compare the 'Beelzebub argument' in all three synoptics is an interesting exercise.

The charge that Jesus worked by the power of the prince of devils was weak and it had to be shown up for the sin that it was. The people who could not distinguish between the work of the Holy Spirit and the superstition of Satanism were in a sorry state. To say that Jesus did good by the power of evil was to admit that there was serious division in Satan's ranks. Jesus's works of healing and mercy were possible only if he had 'bound' the devil and stolen his 'goods'.

What is the 'unforgiveable sin' (v. 31)? This reference has caused many people to worry in case they have commited the sin, but since their concern shows that their conscience is still active, it is a saving grace. It seems that Matthew is purposely linking the saying with the accusation that Jesus was in league with the devil. That would be 'slander against the Holy Spirit'. But it could also refer to a more general loss of moral values and judgement when, like the witches in *Macbeth,* people say that 'fair is foul and foul is fair'. Many who do that do not admit that it is a sin and refuse to acknowledge any need of forgiveness. Perhaps that is what is meant by Jesus in v. 35.

vv. 38–45   Signs and spirits   (Mark 8: 11–12, Luke 11: 29–32)
Jewish leaders were sometimes asked to 'prove' that their teaching was genuine by some kind of sensational 'sign', like fire falling from heaven or a star shooting across the sky. Why the Pharisees demanded such 'signs' when they had witnessed miracles being peformed is a mystery, but Jesus refused the request and suggested that the only 'sign' they would see would be the same that Jonah saw in the repentance of the people of Nineveh.

What did that mean? In the parable about Jonah in the Old Testament (in which, incidentally, the word 'whale' is never mentioned) Jonah was sent to Nineveh, the capital of Assyria, to warn them of the judgements which would come upon them unless they repented. They subsequently repented and God accepted it, much to Jonah's dismay, as he had been looking forward to seeing them punished.

In Luke's version that is the only point he takes from the parable, but Matthew, anxious to turn it into an allegory, sees in it a reference to the resurrection (v. 40), which would be the greatest 'sign' of all, for Jesus was far greater than Jonah.

'The Queen of the South' (v. 42) was the Queen of Sheba who went to listen to Solomon's wisdom (1 Kings 10) and was greatly impressed. But here the crowd were not ready to pay the same attention to Jesus, who was far superior to Solomon.

The parable of the spirits (vv. 43–45) is a short story but has a lot of meaning. A person expels evil thoughts and desires from his mind and thinks he has seen the last of them. But in the desert – thought to be the home of demons – the evil spirits cannot find enough work to do, so they return to the 'vacuum' of the person's mind, which he foolishly had not filled with any other ideas, and they soon take over again. Perhaps Matthew was thinking of the people who had once accepted Jesus but were now doubting him.

vv. 46–50   Jesus's family   (Mark 3: 31–35, Luke 8: 19–21)
The early Church often looked upon itself as the 'family of Christ', so this story had significance for Matthew's readers. Mark says that Jesus's family

arrived 'to take charge of him', probably because they were concerned about his well-being, but Matthew misses that out, emphasizing Jesus's spiritual, rather than actual family, which he later refers to in 13: 55.

Mark says that Jesus pointed to the 'people sitting round him' as his 'family', but Matthew is more specific, saying that Jesus 'pointed to his disciples'.

CHAPTER 13   TEACHING BY PARABLES

This chapter of parables is the nucleus of the 'third section' of this gospel. Mark gives a sample of Jesus's teaching by parables (Chapter 4), which Matthew adapts to illustrate the nature of the Kingdom of Heaven. He expands Mark's four parables to seven, because seven is a sacred number, and points out that most of the parables were addressed to the 'crowds', although there are one or two 'asides' to the disciples.

What is a parable? The word itself comes from a Greek word which literally means 'to compare'. The Greek is a rendering of the Hebrew word 'mashal', which means a proverb or wise saying. So a parable is a way of emphasizing a point that someone is trying to make.

But the purpose of parables is more complex. Though without doubt the most easily remembered parts of Jesus's teaching, his parables are also the most vulnerable in the sense that they are open to all kinds of interpretation. In other words, there is a temptation, and indeed there has often been a tendency, to try to turn the parables into allegories; even the Church is sometimes guilty of this. St Augustine, in particular, joined in this determination to 'decipher' the parables. In the story of the Good Samaritan, for example, he said that the man who journeyed from Jerusalem was Adam, expelled from the holiness of Jerusalem because of his rebellion, the robbers who attacked him were the devil and his angels, who robbed him of his innocence, and so on. That is an extreme example, but it illustrates the point.

If we ask what exactly parables are, if they are not to be taken as allegories, there is no easy answer, but one simple explanation is to say that a parable is a metaphor or simile drawn from everyday life to aid the understanding of a point. For example, it may be said that wealth can be a hindrance to a person in their relationship with God, but if we say, 'It is easier for a camel to pass through the eye of a needle than for a rich man to enter the Kingdom', the point is brought more vividly to life. This idea can easily be developed into a short story or even a full-length drama, like the story of the Prodigal Son.

The important thing to bear in mind is that a parable has one main point of comparison and the details, though they may be colourful, are really secondary. It may or may not be a true story but it contains a moral truth, whereas in an allegory every detail has a hidden meaning. Of course, having said that, there is a danger of giving the parables too simple an explanation; an example would be to say that the parable of the pounds (Luke 19: 11–27) is simply advice on how to invest money wisely or that the story of the vineyard workers (Matthew 20: 1–16) was really a lesson in good labour relations! So, when people talk about the parables as the 'simple gospel', it is really an understatement.

One point to note is that only two of the forty or so parables found in the gospels are explained and these explanations look suspiciously like attempts to allegorize the parables. This may indicate that the explanations are a later insertion.

vv. 1–9   The seed and the soil   (Mark 4: 1–9, Luke 8: 4–8)

After a brief introduction (vv. 1–3) to set the scene, Matthew tells this very true-to-life tale of a farmer planting a crop in his field. (The fields were divided not by hedges but by stones dug up from the soil.) Some of the seed fell on the path along the edge of the field and had no chance to grow, but some survived and produced a crop. The seed represented the different ways in which people responded to the gospel; perhaps Jesus was thinking of his own teaching and the varied response he had received.

The soil   This is described in greater detail than either the sower or the seed; it is the chief element in the parable. Some was hard and indifferent, some stony and shallow, and some in good condition and conducive towards producing a good crop. A hundredfold increase on each seed would be very rare, even though Josephus writes of the 'unusual fertility of the plain of Gennesaret' on the west side of Lake Galilee.

vv. 18–23   The sequel   (Mark 4: 13–20, Luke 8: 11–15)

This parable and the one about the weeds in the wheat were the only two to be given an interpretation, which is probably why Matthew puts them both together in this chapter. Both explanations can be regarded as examples of how the early Church attempted to allegorize the parables, because many scholars believe that the interpretations were later additions made in the light of later events. Since the original occasion on which the parable had been told had been forgotten, and therefore the point the parable was meant to illustrate had also been lost, such interpretations should be considered with some caution.

Thus, in this explanation of the Sower, we find a language and a style unlike the majority of the sayings of Jesus, but very similar to the style of Paul and the other New Testament writers. For example, four of the Greek words used here are not found anywhere else in the synoptic gospels outside this passage, and three other Greek words are used in only one other place. It seems likely, therefore, that what we have here was not part of the original teachings of Jesus but part of the later preaching of the early Church.

This is why, mixed in with the basic point about how the gospel is either understood and received or misunderstood and rejected, are the 'undertones' about persecution and love of personal possessions which were among the problems of the Church. Nevertheless, Matthew is anxious to show that many *did* accept the teaching, and he reverses Mark's order and puts the 'hundredfold' increase first.

vv. 10–17 Why did Jesus speak in parables? (Mark 4: 10–12, Luke 8: 9–10)
Mark and Luke deal with this difficult question only briefly but Matthew expands it because it was an issue very much in the minds of early Christians. Jesus was not the first to use this method, the Old Testament prophets did the same. The usual explanation for such teaching is that in the Middle East 'picture language' was commonly used and a story would be remembered more easily than a sermon. That could be true today of many church services!

However, here Jesus gave a different reason which at first sounds strange but to which the clue seems to be the word 'secrets' in v. 11. The Greek word is 'mysterion', meaning something once secret but now made known to selected people. So the 'secret' of the Kingdom had been given to the disciples and if they were receptive they would be given more (v. 12), but if not it would be lost. The quotation from Isaiah 6: 9–10 seems to indicate that it was God's *plan* that some would respond and some would not, but the original point of the Sower story seems to be that Jesus was far too much of a realist to expect complete success. After all, the main purpose of the parables must have been to clarify the truth, not to conceal it.

The Kingdom of Heaven (v. 11) Matthew alone uses this phrase, some thirty-two times, preferring it to the 'Kingdom of God', which he uses only four times. Jews normally avoided the actual use of God's name by speaking instead of 'heaven'. In the Old Testament the word 'malkuth' meant 'kingship' rather than 'kingdom', in the sense of God's plan and moral purpose for all the earth (Zechariah 14: 9). In the parables of Jesus the Kingdom is likened to some active and present event, with the person and preaching of Jesus showing what it was all about.

vv. 24–30 The weeds in the wheat
Some regard this story, found only in Matthew, as the writer's retelling of the short parable in Mark 4: 26–29, bearing in mind Matthew's habit of 'doubling' certain incidents, as well as his eagerness to answer implied questions. Perhaps he thought Mark's parable needed some explanation.

The intention In the night someone whose sole intention was to spoil the farmer's plan sowed weeds amongst the wheat. The wheat was probably 'darnel', a poisonous plant which not only grew as tall as wheat but looked like it too. In fact, some regarded it as 'perverted' wheat.

The impulse   The servants wanted to deal with the problem there and then, which at first seemed sensible, but the farmer preferred patience. Trampling all over the wheat to take out the tares would not solve the problem, better to wait until the harvest to sort it out.

vv. 36–43   The interpretation
This explanation is even more of an allegory than the one about the Sower and many scholars regarded it as more to do with the problems of the early Church than as a product of the teaching of Jesus. Several points arise from this parable:
1. The problem of evil is not explained, but neither is it ignored. The question must be raised: 'If this is God's world, where does evil come from and who is the enemy of God?' The parable tries to answer this.
2. Good and evil are not always easy to distinguish, sometimes they look alike. The way Satan works in this world is to deceive, not to be openly hostile. That is why he often comes in disguise, as in the second Creation story (Genesis 3). Here, he did not *interfere* with the wheat, he just planted the imitation wheat and left that to do the damage.
3. Christians believe that there *will* be a time of reckoning when everyone will have to account for how they have used their lives. Many forget that.
4. The allegory must not be taken too far. In the story, the wheat and the weeds could not change, but people can. Many a person's life has been changed for the better, which is what the gospel is all about. Conversely, good lives can become evil.

vv. 31–33   Mustard and yeast   (Mark 4: 30–32, Luke 13: 18–21)
Matthew has cleverly combined both Mark's and Luke's accounts, but his botany is a bit awry. The mustard seed was not the smallest and the birds tended to perch on the plant, but not to nest in its branches. It could grow up to 3 metres tall and was more suited to a field than a garden.

Possibly Jesus was thinking of Daniel 4: 20–21, where the Babylonian kingdom was likened to a tree in which birds roosted, but that kingdom collapsed while God's would increase. The message of the parable was one of hope and growth, a great deal from a small beginning, which is so often true of nature and of human nature.

The yeast parable makes the same point, which is why they are together. A small amount of yeast was mixed with three 'seahs' of flour – about 25 kilograms – which would be a lot to 'leaven', but it was done. (Incidentally, this story was often allegorized by the early Church, with the 'three measures' of the original version becoming the Father, Son and Holy Spirit or even the three sons of Noah!)

vv. 44–50   Pearls and fish
This group of three parables is addressed directly to the disciples, since the crowd had been dismissed (v. 36). All three are found only in Matthew.

The treasures   Finding treasure is always a good plot for a story, for it fires the imagination. Here the ethics may seem a bit dubious, with the man wanting to buy the field without telling the owner what was in it, but the point is that the Kingdom is so desirable that no sacrifice is too great.

In the story of the pearl, the merchant may well have had to travel long distances, because the search for precious stones often meant going to the Persian Gulf or to India, but when he found an exceptional pearl, he would give up everything else in order to get it.

The seine-net story, the third parable, would appeal to the disciples. The net was a large vertical fishing net held between two boats; it was sometimes called a drag-net as it was weighted on one edge to keep it vertical. Lake Galilee teemed with fish and all kinds would be caught in the net. When the fishermen got back to the shore they would sort out the fish, keeping the good ones and throwing away the bad. In this sorting out of the genuine from the false a comparison is made with the day of judgement, though the 'fiery furnace' was probably a later addition.

Fishing in Lake Galilee today

vv. 51–52   The ideal disciple

On the surface, this seems to be a statement that a good disciple will live up to the meaning of that word and be a good 'student'. However, some scholars think that here there is a clue to Matthew's identity, like an artist signing his own work. They think he is a scribe, or even a Pharisee, who had become a Christian. In this way, he had taken something 'new' (the gospel) from the 'riches' of the old (the Old Testament).

There have been attempts to 'find' the writers like this in all the gospels. Some think that Mark was the young man who tried to warn Jesus in Gethsemane (Mark 14: 51), that Luke was the companion to Cleopas (Luke 24: 18) and that John was 'the disciple whom Jesus loved' (John 13: 33). Some of these attempts are not very convincing.

vv. 53–58   No honour at Nazareth   (Mark 6: 1–6, Luke 4: 16–30)
The usual 'finishing formula' to the teaching section occurs in v. 53, but Matthew goes on to give a conclusion which sums up the theme in this third section – the acceptance or rejection of Jesus.

The place   Matthew, like Mark, does not actually name the town, as Luke does, but we assume he means Nazareth (although in 4: 13 he said that Jesus had settled at Capernaum). Nazareth is not mentioned in the Old Testament or by Josephus and the name is something of a mystery. It is found in several forms in various manuscripts, including 'Nazarat' and 'Nazara'. It could come from the Hebrew 'nazar', meaning 'to watch', or from 'netzer', meaning 'to sprout' or 'to shoot'.

The preaching   Provided that a person was qualified or competent to speak, the president of the synagogue (such as Jairus, Mark 5: 22) could invite him to read the lesson and then explain the scripture in a sermon. The fact that Jesus was asked to speak and was often addressed as 'Rabbi', which meant 'teacher', indicated that he was regarded as qualified, if not by training, then certainly by his reputation and power as a preacher. One report of his teaching said that 'no one ever spoke like this man' (John 7: 46).

Matthew does not tell us what Jesus spoke about, but he records the amazement of the congregation and the fact that they could think only of him as the 'carpenter's son'.

Doesn't this deny the virgin birth?   There are two translations of this verse in Mark's version. One is 'the carpenter, the son of Mary' and the other is 'the son of the carpenter and Mary', so Matthew plays safe. It does not mean that he has forsaken the virgin birth idea, but to describe someone in those days by his mother's name often meant that there were doubts about the father, so Matthew avoids any difficulties by saying 'son of the carpenter'.

What do we know of Jesus's real family?   Very little. In fact, Christians are divided as to whether 'brothers and sisters' meant blood brothers or not. In the synoptics very little is heard of Mary after the birth story, but John's gospel (19: 25) says she was at the crufixion and Acts 1: 14 says she was with the disciples after the resurrection. All the gospels seem to accept that

The interior of a synagogue in Jerusalem. In the foreground is the bimah, the platform from which the scrolls of the Law are read. In the background is the Holy Ark.

the brothers and sisters mentioned here were his family in the normal sense of the word, but John's gospel indicates that his brothers were not very co-operative or kind (7: 5). Very little is known of the brothers mentioned here, except that James later became the leader of the Church in Jerusalem (Acts 12: 17).

One version of this gospel says that the people of his home town 'rejected' Jesus, but in fact it was indifference rather than hostility. It was the proof of the parable of the Sower: the seed was sown but the soil did not respond.

THE FOURTH SECTION: 14: 1 – 18: 35

In this section the teaching material is in Chapter 18, with Chapters 14–17 leading up to it. Matthew takes Mark's material, from 6: 14 to 9: 32, and adds to it from 'Q'. He shows how Jesus's Messiahship became more apparent and then gives the authority of Jesus's teaching as a guide for those who were faced with particular problems in the early Church.

CHAPTER 14

vv. 1–12   The beheading of the Baptist   (Mark 6: 14–29, Luke 9: 7–9)
Matthew seems to see this event as a prelude to the fate that Jesus would face.

The intrigue   The story has a plot worthy of a popular detective novel, but both Matthew and Mark seem a bit confused about the 'clues'. The facts were that Herod Antipas was the Tetrarch, or ruler, of Galilee from 4 B.C to A.D. 39. He was a son of Herod the Great and Malthace, a Samaritan and a wife of Herod. Antipas had apparently married the daughter of an Arabian King, Aretas, but later fell in love with Herodias, wife of his half-brother, Herod Philip (not to be confused with Philip the tetrarch, another brother) and married her. John the Baptist had protested that according to Leviticus 20: 21, this marriage was illegal and he had been imprisoned for his pains. Mark says that Herod liked to talk to John, but Matthew says that Herod wanted to kill him. Matthew's version is borne out by Josephus, who says that Herod murdered John because he feared the Baptist might start some kind of rebellion. Josephus makes no mention of the incident recorded here.

The story may well have been coloured by market-place gossip about 'goings-on' at the palace and possibly exaggerated by ideas from the Book of Esther, but one thing is clear: John's protest cost him his life. When he criticized Antipas he knew the risks he ran but he did not hesitate. Like Jeremiah and Jesus, John's courage was to cost him dear.

When John's disciples went to tell Jesus (v. 12), they must have been wondering what had happened to moral justice in the world. They had always believed that, according to the Psalms, God was 'the strength and shield of the righteous', yet Herod, the evil man, was still alive and John was dead. It did not make sense and no doubt they 'went to tell Jesus' how they felt.

vv. 13–33   Miracles and marvels   (Mark 6: 30–44, Luke 9: 10–17, John 6: 1–15)
Matthew now recounts two incidents to introduce two important elements in the early Church: the Lord's Supper and what he saw as the part played by Peter in the organization of the Church.

vv. 13–21   The miraculous meal
This is the only miracle to be recorded in all four gospels. In the commentary on Mark's gospel we saw that there have been many 'explanations' for 'The Feeding of the Five Thousand'. Whatever interpretation is taken, the fact remains that this was a most important

event because it was a very testing time for Jesus. John (6: 15) says that it was an attempt by the people to persuade Jesus to be their leader. If they were Zealots, as they may well have been, they would have wanted Jesus to be the kind of political Messiah suggested in the third temptation (4: 8).

Many scholars think that Matthew is drawing a resemblance to the Last Supper or even anticipating it. Jesus gave a blessing, as he did at the Supper, and he broke the bread in the same way and gave it to the disciples to give to the crowd. In the early Church this miracle was known as 'the lonely sacrament', and there is little doubt that it was believed to be connected with the Last Supper, as well as with the story of Moses feeding the people with bread in the wilderness (Exodus 16).

In John's version it is a boy who provides the bread and fishes, but Matthew does not mention him. Matthew is the only one to anticipate the question that many would ask, as to whether there were only five thousand *men*, as all the other gospels say, and no families, so he adds, 'besides women and children'.

vv. 22–33 Walking on the water (Mark 6: 45–52, John 6: 16–21)

One of the features of this gospel is its emphasis on the place of Peter in the gospel story and, as far as Matthew's readers would be concerned, in the early Church too. That is why Matthew expands this incident so dramatically. Both Mark and John, after describing the fears of the disciples, say that Jesus climbed into the boat and the wind dropped. However, in Matthew's account Peter tries to imitate Jesus by attempting to walk on the water as well.

What did the miracle mean? To try to 'explain' it by saying that Jesus was walking *by* the water or on some kind of sandbank is not satisfactory. In fact, it is unnecessary to explain it, because to do so is to miss the point. Some see the incident as a 'foretaste' of a resurrection appearance, or a glimpse into the kind of spirit world of which Jesus was a part. The important aspect, however, is that although Peter made a brave attempt to follow Jesus's example, his faith turned to fear and Jesus had to help him. No doubt many of Matthew's readers would see the connection between this and Peter's later boast (26: 35) that he would die for Jesus but his subsequent denial, through fear, that he had ever known him.

vv. 34–36 Recognition and response

Gennesaret, to the north-west of Lake Galilee, was a plain so 'perfect' that it was sometimes called 'the garden of princes'. It was certainly fertile as far as response to Jesus was concerned, though the emphasis seems to be on healing rather than teaching. Like the woman with haemorrhages (9: 20), even those who touched only the fringe of his robe were healed.

CHAPTER 15

vv. 1–20   What really defiles?   (Mark 7: 1–23)

In Chapter 15 Matthew resumes his discussion of questions which concerned the Church. He starts with 'defilement' and Jesus's attitude towards it. Probably underlying this incident was the later argument about whether non-Jewish converts to Christianity should be bound by Jewish laws, a matter of some controversy in the Church at Jerusalem (Acts 15).

The issue   It centred around a reluctance on the part of the disciples to wash their hands before a meal. This was not a written law, and it was for reasons not of hygiene but of purity. At one time it was an obligation only for priests but it had come to be expected of everyone. Hands had to be washed before eating in order to be free from 'defilement', of which there could be many causes.

The implications   It was tricky ground and Jesus had to tread carefully, but his answer was firm. He reminded his critics that there were other ways of breaking the commandments and that *they* were guilty of some of them, though most Jews of his day would probably have regarded the punishment of death for disobeying parents (Exodus 21: 17) as unnecessarily drastic. Jesus seems to be condemning people who, instead of providing for their parents, asserted that all their belongings were promised to God – probably as a gift to the Temple – and were therefore not available to help their parents. This, he said, was far worse than not washing hands.

The indignation (v. 12)   Peter is spotlighted as the spokesman and he asks for an explanation. Was Jesus advocating a relaxation of all the laws dealing with 'unclean' foods, as set out in Leviticus 11? Was he saying that it no longer mattered 'what went into a person's mouth' (v. 11)? This, to many Jews, would be unthinkable, which is no doubt why Peter said that the Pharisees had taken 'great offence' (v. 12).

Jesus made it clear that some of the things regarded as traditional were not of God's planting and should be 'rooted up'; those who still taught them were blind guides. This reference is to a sight, not uncommon in those days, of a line of blind people being led by someone who was supposed to be able to see.

Mark gives a list of thirteen vices which 'pollute' a person's life, but Matthew selects only seven, a number he uses frequently.

Discussion Point

Whatever the social customs or traditions, some things we eat or drink or take into our bodies can do a lot of harm. The same applies to what goes into our minds through what we read or see or hear. In what ways can television programmes, films, books, conversations, etc., sometimes prove to be mental 'food' that can cause moral 'sickness'?

vv. 21–31   Sheep and dogs   (Mark 7: 24–30)

Matthew has changed this story somewhat from Mark's version to show that faith can overcome prejudice and tradition. Mark does not mention the woman's faith.

The scene   Mark implies that Jesus left Galilee to go up to Tyre because he wanted to get away from all the controversy and criticism, and to get a much needed rest. To do that, he wanted to remain unrecognized, but the Syro-Phoenician woman found him. Matthew calls her a 'Canaanite'. This is not geographically correct, but he may be using it in the Old Testament sense of 'someone of pagan religion': he wants to contrast her faith with the doubts of some of the Jews.

The silence   Few stories have caused more comment than this one and many attempts have been made to explain its difficulties. According to Matthew Jesus did not enter any house in Tyre, he did not seem very anxious to help the woman at first and the disciples seemed decidedly unfriendly towards her.

However, several points need to be made:
1. Jesus's silence (v. 23) need not have indicated indifference. He was also silent before Herod (Luke 23: 9) and before Pilate (Matthew 27: 14). So this was probably a silence in which Jesus was searching for the right answer.
2. At no time in the gospels is Jesus shown as being unkind or discourteous towards women, so why should he be so to this one?
3. Although many Jews were contemptuous of the Romans, as oppressors, most did not extend this attitude to all foreigners. Jesus may well have been using a phrase which some Jews applied to some foreigners to show the contrast between his attitude and theirs.

The fact remains that the daughter was cured – one of the very few healings from a distance – and the mother's faith was commended.

The incident was followed by other miracles of healing (vv. 29–31) which may have also have been among gentiles, since Matthew says that they gave thanks to the 'God of Israel'.

vv. 32–39   The further feeding   (Mark 8: 1–10)

This is one of the stories that Luke does not copy from Mark, perhaps because he thought it was a duplicate of the Feeding of the Five Thousand, but there are enough differences to indicate that it was a separate occasion. Matthew copies it without comment and with very little attempt to 'edit' it, except, after saying there were four thousand men present, adding 'to say nothing of women and children'. This is the same phrase that he used earlier.

'Magadan' (v. 39) is difficult to identify, except to say that it seems to have been on the west shore of Lake Galilee.

CHAPTER 16

vv. 1–12   Signs of the times   (Mark 8: 11–13, Luke 12: 54–56)
The demand (vv. 1–4)   As in 12: 38, there was a request for a 'sign' and again Jesus referred to Jonah. Matthew says that both the Pharisees and the Sadducees came, but besides being unfriendly towards each other, the Sadducees were based at the temple in Jerusalem and would be unlikely to live in Galilee. Matthew has evidently linked them together to emphasize the combined influence against which Jesus was to warn the disciples.

The deadly 'leaven'   The word could be used to mean either influence or secrecy; here Jesus seemed to use it in both senses. He was referring to the teachings of the religious leaders as hidden, yet not good. It was also a play on words since dough could mean dullness, which perhaps applied to the disciples at that time.

It should be remembered that Jesus's criticism of some of the religious leaders was aimed at their inclination to think that obeying certain laws and doing good deeds was all that religion demanded. This meant that they did not have a true relationship with God, because they tended to think that a person could be 'saved' by the Law rather than by faith. Many Christians still confuse this issue; Paul, in his letter to the Romans, has a lot to say about it.

vv. 13–20   Peter's recognition   (Mark 8: 27–30, Luke 9: 18–21)
Matthew takes this material from Mark, but adds to it words not found anywhere else in the gospels (vv. 17–19) and about which there has been a great deal of debate and disagreement.

Something that might help our study here is what scholars call 'form criticism'. Put simply, this is the study of 'units of tradition', which are incidents with their own individual background, or history, but whose background is not now known. Each gospel writer takes these units and uses them in a way most suited to his own particular purpose. Such a unit is what we call 'Peter's confession' and Matthew uses it not only to show that Jesus was recognized as the Messiah, as the other synoptic writers do, but also to show that Peter was given authority in the early Church.

The place   Mark says that this happened 'on the way' to Caesarea Philippi, while Matthew maintains it was when they arrived in that area, though neither says that Jesus actually entered the town. It was a place at the foot of Mount Hermon and near the source of the River Jordan. It had long been associated with the worship of the Roman god Pan, and was called Paneas before it was enlarged by Herod Philip and its name changed to Caesarea in honour of the Roman Emperor. ('Philippi' was added to the name to distinguish it from the port of Caesarea.) In fact, since the reason for going to this 'pagan' place is not given, it might be suggested that it was the intention of the gospel writers to show the difference between the worship of the pagan god and the recognition of Jesus as the true Messiah.

The prophets (v. 14)   Matthew adds Jeremiah to the list, probably because many people saw a similarity between Jesus and that Old Testament prophet. For example, Jeremiah spoke of a 'new covenant' (31: 31) and he protested at the temple (Ch. 7).

The question   Jesus first asked what the other people were saying about him and the disciples gave him answers which indicated that the people thought he was equal to the best of the Old Testament prophets. Then he asked what *they* thought and Peter gave his memorable reply: 'You are the Messiah'.

What did he mean by that?   Different groups understood the term 'Messiah' in different ways, but basically it meant a figure who would bring peace and justice through the gaining of political power and popularity. Certainly, he would be a victorious figure for whom the idea of defeat and suffering would be foreign. (This is in contrast to the 'suffering servant' image of the second Isaiah.)

The puzzle   In Mark's account Jesus did not admit or deny Peter's declaration, but according to Matthew he immediately commended Peter for his suggestion and reminded him what the name 'Petros' meant. The question is whether Jesus was giving Simon a new 'image' – because in the Bible a change of name often meant a change of character – or whether he was making him the future leader of the Church. Does 'rock' refer to Peter as a person or to his faith and insight in recognizing Jesus as the Messiah?
  Several points need to be borne in mind:
1. Matthew was very keen to answer questions which he knew would be in many people's minds. One was whether or not Jesus was really the Messiah. Mark *implies* that he was, but Matthew wants to make it clear.
2. This gospel almost certainly first circulated in Syria, where Peter's importance was of great interest to the readers since he was a leading figure in the introduction of Christianity to that country.
3. There is a text in Isaiah (28: 16) about 'laying a stone in Zion'. Was Matthew thinking of that?
4. Did Peter subsequently live up to his 'reputation' as a 'rock'? Jesus was to call him 'Satan', and Paul, writing to the Galatians (2: 11–14), seemed to think that Kephas, as he called him, was anything *but* a rock!
  In my view, Christ is the real and only foundation stone of the Church and the fact that God can use people like Peter, Paul, James, John or anyone else as further 'stones' is a matter for rejoicing, not for recriminations.

vv. 21–28   The conditions of service   (Mark 8: 31 – 9: 1, Luke 9: 22–27)
Jesus then made the first prediction of his 'passion'. (The word comes from the Latin 'passus', a form of the verb 'to suffer'.) Peter was horrified at the

idea of the Messiah suffering defeat and death and he took Jesus aside to tell him that he had got it all wrong. To Jesus Peter was 'Satan' or tempter (v. 23), tempting him to be the very kind of Messiah that he never intended to be.

Then Jesus made it quite clear. He was not that kind of Messiah, so anyone who wanted to be his follower must forget any ideas of 'victory'. In fact, they must take up a cross and 'lose' their lives. That didn't mean dying for him so much as living for him, putting self-interest and self-indulgence to 'death' by forgetting self. Selfishness is the starting-point of so many sins and to 'trade in' the soul for temporary satisfaction is to make a bad bargain.

CHAPTER 17   VISIONS AND VOICES

vv. 1–8   The transfiguration   (Mark 9: 2–13, Luke 9: 28–36)

This event is so-called because the literal meaning of the original Greek word is 'to change in appearance'. No doubt Matthew would have in mind the experience of Moses when he went up Mount Sinai with three named men and seventy leaders of Israel and then went on alone into the cloud where God spoke to him; when he came down his face 'shone' (Exodus 24: 9–18, 34: 30). The main point was that Peter had 'confessed' that Jesus was the Messiah and now the 'voice from heaven' was confirming it.

Why did Moses and Elijah appear?   The Greek word in v. 3 for 'appear' literally means 'vision', so exactly what happened is hard to say. But the significance is that Moses represented the Law or Torah and Elijah the prophets, and the voice told the disciples to listen to Jesus as the divine authority, meaning that he was greater than either Moses or Elijah. According to Malachi 4: 5, Elijah was expected to appear again to herald the coming of the Messiah. The 'shelters' (v. 4) may have been a reminder that God would pitch his tent, or 'tabernacle', with his people, as he had done in the wilderness (Exodus 40: 1).

vv. 9–13   Down to earth

The question in the minds of the disciples, when they remembered Malachi's prophecy was, 'If Jesus is the Messiah, why did Elijah not come?' Matthew expands on Mark's version to make the answer clearer: Elijah *had* come, in the form of John the Baptist, but he had not been recognized as the forerunner.

vv. 14–20   Faith and failings   (Mark 9: 14–29, Luke 9: 37–43)

Mark indicates that the boy was an epileptic and Matthew makes this clear (v. 15), but he misses out Mark's claim that the father had 'some faith'. He wants to contrast the power of Jesus and the faithlessness of an 'unbelieving generation'. Even the faith of the disciples was too small, which was a disappointment because they had been given the authority to heal (10: 1).

vv. 22–23 Second prediction of death (Mark 9: 30–32, Luke 9: 44–45)
These three 'warnings' – 20: 17–19 is the third in this gospel – are like the 'solemn strokes of a tolling bell', as one writer has put it. Matthew is kinder to the disciples than Mark is. He does not say that they 'did not understand', but that they were 'filled with grief'.

vv. 24–27 Tax-collecting!
This is a strange story, but I do not think a miracle or even a mystery is intended. The temple tax was a half-shekel due from all free male Jews over twenty years of age and was paid six weeks before Passover. There was little indication that many objected to paying it and Jesus makes it clear here that taxes should be paid, both civil and religious. This seems to be another example of Matthew drawing attention to Peter.

CHAPTER 18 PROBLEMS AND PARABLES

Matthew has now reached the 'teaching' part of his fourth section and he deals with certain 'community problems' in the early Church. Chapters 14–17 have shown how a new kind of freedom was beginning to emerge, but freedom could be a fragile thing and could easily be abused. So the problems centred around how the Church should regard wrongdoers and wrongdoing, how much it should compromise with what seemed to be falling standards, and how it should deal with the 'weak' and those who were 'young in faith'. Matthew suggests some solutions.

vv. 1–4 Cause for concern (Mark 9: 33–37, 42–48, Luke 9: 46–48, 17: 1–2)
The first issue is the place and importance of young people in the Church. Matthew brings together a collection of Jesus's teaching to give some guidance.

The request The matter arose out of an argument amongst the disciples about being the 'greatest' in the kingdom. Evidently they were thinking of influence and position in some kind of earthly kingdom. So Jesus used a child to illustrate the meaning of greatness. It was a matter of being childlike, not childish, and the qualities needed were trust, dependence and a sense of wonder, the essential elements of childhood.

The reponsibility Jesus then referred to a group who are young not only in years but also in faith and may well be exploited. The Church's task was to make sure that no stumbing-block was put in their path, by example or by neglect. The 'millstone' (v. 6) was so large that an animal was needed to turn it and to be 'drowned in the sea' would deny a person a proper burial, which to many Jews would be a dreadful fate.

The remedy (vv. 9–10)   Sometimes a person has to lose a limb in order to save a life, but Jesus was drawing a parallel with moral mutilations, the temptations and habits which need drastic treatment if they are to be successfully overcome.

What are 'guardian angels'? (v. 10)   It was thought that people had guardian angels to protect them from harm, as in Peter's release from prison (Acts 12: 7). The problem was that this seemed to work for some people and not for others. Certainly, today, when there is so much cruelty and neglect of children, it could be asked what has happened to some of their 'guardian angels'!

vv. 12–14   Sheep and strays   (Luke 15: 3–7)
Luke uses this story to illustrate God's concern over the 'lost', but Matthew uses it to show what the attitude should be towards those young people – and perhaps older people – who may be 'lost' to the Church through neglect or sin. The main concern should be for the 'strayed' rather than for the 'safe'. Possibly Jesus had in mind the parable of Ezekiel about the lost sheep (Ezekiel 34).

A shepherd with his flock of sheep in the Golan

vv. 15–35   Faults and forgiveness
What to do about Christians who committed serious sins was a practical problem in the Church, as can be seen from some of Paul's letters (e.g. Romans 2: 3). Many solutions were suggested.

80

vv. 15–18   Trying times

Although the wisdom is from Jesus, some wonder whether the actual words 'treat him like a tax-collector' were really his, particularly in view of the way he himself treated people like Zacchaeus (Luke 19). However, the point here is the question of patience. It was essential to try to sort out problems privately, in a spirit of love and brotherhood, and moreover, to keep on trying. If in the end there was no response, then little else could be done.

Verse 17 is only the second time in the gospels that the word 'Church' is used. The first occurrence is also in Matthew (16: 18). The Greek word is 'ekklesia', which in the states of Greece meant an assembly summoned for legal purposes, but in the New Testament it meant a congregation of believers. At no time did it refer to a building, which is in some people's idea of a 'Church'.

vv. 19–22   The mathematics of mercy

Matthew starts with the very simple numbers of two and three (vv. 19–20) to show that even a small congregation could multiply the Holy Spirit and that those who meet in faith could be sure of Christ's presence with them.

Then, still on numbers, he records that Peter asked how many times he should forgive a wrongdoer. Peter had worked out that what he thought was a very generous estimate – seven being a 'perfect' number in Judaism – but was told that although his calculations were correct his estimate was much too low. Forgiveness is an exercise in mercy, not in mathematics. There should be no limit on love. Some translations have 'seventy times seven', others have 'seventy-seven times', but the real point is that it is not a sum to be done in the head but in the heart!

vv. 23–35   The two debtors

Matthew ends this 'teaching section' with a story found only in his gospel – from the 'M' source – and which sums up the teaching very well. There is no attempt to allegorize. It contains one simple point: the need to forgive as we ourselves are forgiven.

The debt   The amount the man owed was tremendous; the original version says 'ten thousand talents'. If the talents were of silver it would have been an amazing debt for the man to have run up, and if of gold it would have been astronomical! Most translations put it as 'millions of pounds'. The amount is obviously exaggerated in order to emphasize the enormity of the debt which the king was prepared to write off for one man, and also to show the contrast between that and the tiny fraction of that amount – one six-hundred-thousandth part – owed by the servant to his colleague.

The decision   There was a great contrast of attitude as well as amount. The first man had merely asked the king to be patient for the payment and had been told to forget the whole lot, but the other had begged for time to pay and had been thrown into prison. Having written off the debt, the king could easily have regarded his part in the affair as finished, but he was not only generous, he was just. He knew he had to set an example for others to follow and therefore, although he was prepared to forgive a debt, he was not prepared to forgive unforgivingness.

Is this a true picture of God?   Why not? The Lord's Prayer says 'Forgive us our debts', but do we really try to calculate how much we owe? The number of times we are forgiven by God, compared to the times we forgive others, is considerable. How can God forgive us if we are not prepared either to forgive or to ask for forgiveness? The door is closed. The king forgave the first man not because of any goodness in the man, but because he wanted to show the man what forgiveness was all about. There were no half-measures, the man was told to forget the lot. Therefore he owed the king an even greater debt, which was for him to be equally forgiving to someone else. It was *that* debt which he could not pay.

THE FIFTH SECTION: CHAPTERS 19–25

After the usual formula for ending the teaching (19: 1), Matthew begins his fifth section, which is sometimes described as the one on 'Justice and Judgement'. In this section the gospel moves to its tremendous climax in the teaching of Chapters 24 and 25, with the last chapters of the gospel telling of the final drama in the life of Jesus.

The final parable in Chapter 25 is about judgement and to prepare for it Matthew gives the 'judgement' of Jesus on such subjects as marriage and divorce, and rewards. This leads into the last week in the life of Jesus, which ends not only in the judgement *on* Jesus, but also *his* judgement on those who chose to reject him. The writer does all this very carefully, using most of Mark's material in the process.

CHAPTER 19

vv. 3–12   The dilemma of divorce   (Mark 10: 1–12)

The writer raised this question in 5: 31–32, so why do so again? It may be because here he is copying more exactly from Mark, but probably it is because he wants to expand a very important issue, which was whether or not Jesus agreed with either of the two main beliefs on the matter, held by Rabbi Hillel and Rabbi Shammai.

Jesus lifted the whole matter on to a fresh plain from which certain views should be seen. For example:
1. Human beings are capable of a very special kind of love, which is much deeper than just physical attraction. When a man and woman leave their homes to marry, they become 'one' in personalities as well as body. Such a bond is much more than biological.

2. The law said that only the man could divorce the woman directly, not the other way round (though a woman could go to court to request a divorce), but Jesus said that women should have their own rights and equality with men.

3. The permanency of marriage is God's purpose and divorce is not part of that plan.

The objection (v. 7)   So why was divorce allowed (Deuteronomy 24: 1)?

The answer (v. 8)   It was because of the inability of the people to understand God's intentions that divorce was unwillingly permitted rather than actually encouraged.

Was Jesus forbidding marriage after divorce?   It seems that in effect he was saying, 'I will not agree to divorce except for very specific reasons'. Whether he was saying that divorce gave a right to remarry is not clear. One point which may help is that the Greek word used here for 'unchastity' (v. 9) is 'porneia', which means 'continued promiscuity', not just a single case of unfaithfulness. So he may have meant that if a marriage was ended because of persistent betrayal of the bond, remarriage was permissable for the offended party.

The main point to bear in mind is that Jesus was putting forward an important principle: in marriage a man and a woman fulfil the intentions God had when he made them 'male and female', because real human love is a reflection of God's love.

Another objection (vv. 10–12)   The disciples wondered whether, with all these difficulties, it might be better not to marry at all! Here, Matthew is suggesting the kind of question many people would raise, and he uses it to air the whole matter of celibacy.

Some do not marry because, for various reasons, they are incapable. Others think that marriage can distract a person from total commitment to God's cause. Some regard celibacy as a kind of self-denial or even a hardship they endure in order to 'mortify the flesh'. Paul, in his letter to the Church at Corinth (1 Corinthians 7), has something to say on the matter of celibacy which has, to say the least, caused a lot of controversy!

It is a useful exercise to consider why certain religious orders insist that their priests remain unmarried. What are the advantages and disadvantages?

vv. 13–15   Children   (Mark 10: 13–16, Luke 18: 15–17)

Discussion on divorce leads on to the rights of children. Most Jews placed a high value on family life. Among the people who were following Jesus, the parents, or perhaps just the mothers, wanted their children to come into contact with Jesus. The disciples thought that he would not want to be bothered with children, which earned them a strong rebuke. The laying-on of hands in blessing is a beautiful touch to the story.

vv. 16–26   Money matters   (Mark 10: 17–31, Luke 18: 18–30)

Having looked at family life, Matthew now investigates another important issue for Christians – wealth and possessions. He uses the story of the 'rich young ruler' (if we combine the descriptions of the man from all three synoptics) to introduce a subject which was causing a lot of concern.

The inquiry   It was a stock question, often debated in various schools of thought. The lawyer in Luke 10: 25 asked the same thing.

Mark says that the man addressed Jesus as 'Good Master', which prompted Jesus to ask, 'Why do you call me good?'. Matthew carefully avoids such complications!

'Eternal life' (v. 16) did not mean everlasting existence so much as a quality of life which would eventually merit an entry into the Kingdom.

The implications   It was a question on which the man might have expected a lively discussion and lengthy debate, but Jesus's reply must have seemed very ordinary. It was just a reminder about keeping the Commandments, which the man had always done in any case. So what else was expected of him?

Matthew does not give Mark's comment that Jesus looked at the man and 'loved' him. From that it seems that Jesus must have admired him, but he also realized that such commandment-keeping had never really cost the man very much. If he had never been poor or had a bad home life, being honest and honouring his parents had probably been much easier for him than it might have been for someone in different circumstances. When Jesus asked him to do something that was really difficult and would have meant real self-denial, he could not do it. He wanted to be a follower on his own terms.

Is this a rule for discipleship?   To 'sell all' is not possible or practical for most people, but the principle of sacrificing whatever would hinder real dedication is very important. Wealth can sometimes be a hindrance, as Jesus pointed out when the young man had gone.

The camel (v. 24)   Jesus's remarks about the camel and the needle's eye caused the disciples to be amazed and have caused a lot of controversy ever since. Some say that Jesus was misquoted and that the word was 'kamilos', which meant 'cable', not 'camel', or that the 'needle's eye' was the name of a narrow opening in the wall of Jerusalem. Whatever the details, the point is simple. A person who devotes his whole life to the possession of riches will, by his own actions, find it very difficult to enter the Kingdom.

Jesus's whole attitude towards wealth must be considered with caution. There is no indication that his teaching was based on any resentment of riches. It was Paul (1 Timothy 6: 10), not Jesus, who said, 'Love of money is the root of all evil'. But Jesus made it very clear that the making and spending of money can become such an attractive aim that life's real targets are forgotten.

vv. 27–30 'What about us?'

Peter posed the obvious question. The young man had refused to give up his possessions, but what about those who had done so? Many early Christians had 'left all' to follow Jesus: what would *they* get? The answer was that for the disciples there would be special places in the Kingdom and for the rest a repayment 'many times over'. But 'rewards' are not automatic (v. 30)!

CHAPTER 20

vv. 1–16 Trouble at pay-time

To clarify this idea of 'rewards' Matthew records a parable, found only in his gospel, about some workers who grumbled because their boss was too generous – an unusual event! Many people have tried to find an allegory in this parable. For example, the early church scholar Gregory said that the three-hour intervals represented the periods of Jewish history, the men who worked all day were the prophets and those who came in at the last hour were the disciples. But again, the central truth seems so simple that we might miss it: any 'reward' for a person's actions in life is entirely dependent on God's grace and mercy and not on the person's own merit.

The employer He was a landowner who wanted workers for his vineyard. As was the practice, he hired them on a daily basis. The Law (Deuteronomy 24: 15) said he must pay each one at the end of each day 'for he is poor and his heart is set on his wage'. The usual wage for a day's work was a silver coin called a 'denarius'.

The envy This was an unusual hiring because some workers started at 6 a.m., some at 9 a.m. and so on throughout the day. The reaction when the pay-out came was 'It isn't fair', but to whom was it not fair? None received less than they had agreed to and most got much more than they had expected. So why were the full-time workers not happy at the good fortune of their fellow workers? Why, as the master put it (v. 16), were they jealous because he was generous?

The essentials No one pretends that this parable is an exercise in industrial relations. If people were paid as much for working only on a Friday afternoon as for working a full week, the country's economy would soon be in ruins. But it is certainly an insight into human nature and into the way God regards any work done for him.

The reward given to the workers had nothing to do with the number of hours worked but everything to do with the quality of work done. The men who had worked only a short time were not idlers, they had simply not had the chance to work. But once the opportunity was given, they were as faithful and conscientious as the rest, and it was for that they were rewarded. It may not be man's idea of merit, but it is God's.

That is why the 'punch line' to the parable is v. 15, not v. 16 as many assume. God is free to reward as he chooses and it is not up to any of the workers to try to dictate the terms. Some people work all their lives for God, some come late into his service. It is not a matter of waiting until one is old, but of taking the opportunity when it arises.

vv. 17–19   The third prediction of death   (Mark 10: 32–34, Luke 18: 31–34)
This one is fuller and more candid than the other two; the crucifixion is mentioned for the first time.

vv. 20–28   A rash request   (Mark 10: 35–45)
Mark says that James and John asked the favour themselves, Matthew says it was their mother who asked. Whoever it was, it is evident that they had not understood Jesus's remarks on true service, nor had they comprehended what he meant by the Kingdom. They were thinking of self-importance and chief places in some kind of political kingdom.

That was why Jesus, no doubt sadly, told them that they had no idea what they were asking. They may have been thinking of the 'cup of success' of Psalm 23: 5, but he was thinking of a cup of suffering, such as Psalm 73: 10. We know that James was later beheaded by Herod (Acts 12: 2) and there is a strong tradition that John too was martyred.

The mother (v. 20) is not named, but if the women in Matthew 27: 56 are the same as those in Mark 15: 40, then her name was Salome.

The reaction (vv. 24–28)   The others were indignant at the brothers' motives, rather than their misunderstanding, so Jesus gave them another talk on 'greatness'. The Greek word used for 'servant' is the source of the word 'deacon', so a 'minister' should be a servant.

vv. 29–34   Double vision   (Mark 10: 46–52, Luke 18: 35–43)
This is the last stage on the journey to Jerusalem and this is the last miracle, so Matthew makes the most of it.

Mark says there was one man, named as 'Bartimaeus'. Matthew says there were two and mentions no names. It could be that Matthew has a different story because Jesus may well have healed more than one blind man at Jericho. Alternatively, since Mark says that Jesus healed the man as he was leaving the town but Luke says it was as he was entering it, that could be the reason for Matthew doubling the number. An important point is that, while Mark mentions the man's faith, Matthew concentrates on Jesus being 'deeply moved' with pity.

CHAPTERS 21–23   EVENTS IN JERUSALEM

In addition to showing how Jesus went to face the 'opposition' he knew he would encounter in Jerusalem, Matthew includes in this section some teaching which may not have been given at that time but which fits in with his purpose.

Had Jesus been to Jerusalem before? Mark tells of only one visit and Luke and Matthew follow that pattern (apart from Luke's account of Jesus's visit when he was twelve), but John's gospel gives several visits. The synoptics, however, indicate that Jesus was known in the city and it is very unlikely that he would not have been there before this last week. Possibly Mark condenses into one week events which in fact occurred over a longer period.

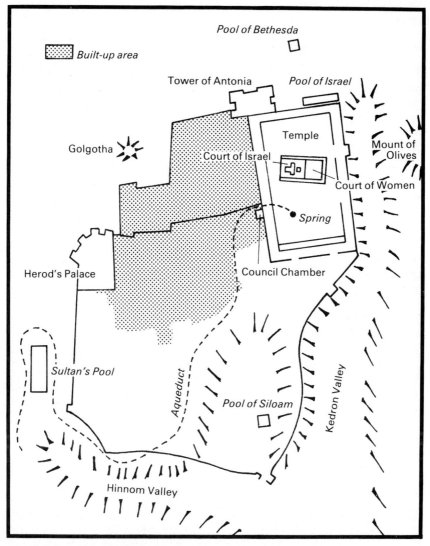

Jerusalem in New Testament times

Perhaps a more pertinent question is why Jesus went there at all, knowing the potential hostility. Apart from the events fulfilling God's purpose, perhaps Jesus wanted to do what so many of the prophets had done – to challenge the nation's leaders and to offer them a new way of life.

CHAPTER 21

vv. 1–11   The 'palm' procession   (Mark 11: 1–11, Luke 19: 28–40, John 12: 12–19)

This is called 'Palm Sunday' because John's gospel says the branches were of palm trees and records the previous day as being six days before Passover (12: 1). 'Bethphage' means 'house of figs'. The two disciples were most probably James and John. Obviously, careful arrangements had been made beforehand, probably by Jesus.

One donkey or two?   The crowd became excited because they remembered the prophecy of Zechariah 9: 9 and that kings, like David and Solomon, had ridden into Jerusalem on a royal mule. Moreover, when Jehu was made king, the people 'spread their garments in front of him' (2 Kings 9: 13).
But Matthew has a problem with the prophecy from Zechariah. He knows that two animals are mentioned (though it is a standard feature of Hebrew poetry to repeat a word in a slightly different form), so he mentions two animals here, though which one Jesus rode is not stated.

Why did Jesus do this?
There are various suggestions:
1. To fulfil the prophecy and to show that he *was* the Messiah.
2. He had no intention of it being a demonstration, but it got a bit out of hand when some spectators became over-enthusiastic.
3. He was persuaded to make the ride by people who wanted to honour him as a prophet (v. 11).
4. It was planned as a challenge to the authorities in Jerusalem. But if that was so, why was it not mentioned at his trials?
5. He was making it clear that although he *was* king, it was not in any pompous or political sense (v. 5).
The last point seems to me the most likely.

vv. 12–17   The temple protest   (Mark 11: 15–19, Luke 19: 45–48, John 2: 13–22)

According to Mark this was the following day, but both Luke and Matthew seem to imply that it happened on the same day as the riding into the city since they do not say it was the next day. Matthew misses out Mark's vital verse about a 'house of prayer for all nations', possibly to put emphasis on the dishonesty and desecration, rather than the discrimination. He sees the main target of the protest as the lack of reverence for the temple as a house of God and the use of the place to make money rather than to do God's work (vv. 14–16).

What did Jesus hope to achieve by this?   He could hardly have expected to stop the sharp practice or to change what had become a custom, but he could remind the people of the fact that Jeremiah had denounced the misuse of the temple (Jeremiah 7: 11) and that Malachi (3: 2) had said that the Lord would come to his temple 'like a refiner's fire'. The Romans later destroyed the building in A.D. 70.

vv. 18–22   Figs and faith   (Mark 11: 12–14)
Matthew says that this occurred 'next morning', which, according to Mark's 'diary', would have been the Tuesday. It is an odd story and many scholars see it as a kind of dramatized version of the parable in Luke 13: 6–9, where Israel is like a fig tree which would not bear fruit.

vv. 23–27   Arguments about authority   (Mark 11: 27–33, Luke 20: 1–8)
The religious leaders now seemed to be determined to get rid of Jesus but they were not prepared to arrest him openly because he was so popular, so they tried to trick him into saying things for which they could criticize him.

By their question, they probably hoped to trap him into saying he was some kind of king, in which case they would have reported him to the Romans as a revolutionary, or that he claimed power from God, in which case they would have accused him of blasphemy. But his counter-question caught them unawares. To have said that John's authority came from God would have made Jesus ask why they had not accepted him and to have denied it would have gone against public opinion.

vv. 28–32   The two sons
This is another 'vineyard' parable, a type of which Matthew seems fond. One son said he would help his father, but did not put his promise into practice, the other said he was not interested, yet he responded.

The point seems plain. It is not what we say but what we actually do that counts. There is a world of difference between lip-service and true service. Some profess to do God's work without doing so, others do not appear to be religious but are in fact very good examples of the gospel.

vv. 33–46   The tenants   (Mark 12: 1–12, Luke 20: 9–19)
This story is more of an allegory than a parable and some scholars are sceptical of it belonging to the original teaching of Jesus.

The symbolism   It is really an adaptation of the vineyard parable of Isaiah 5: 1–7. Various interpretations are possible. For example, the owner may represent God, the vineyard Israel and the tenants the Jewish religious

Part of the Western Wall in Jerusalem, believed to be the remains of Herod's temple

leaders. The servants seem to be the Old Testament prophets, though there are very few instances of any being put to death. The son, of course, is Jesus.

The stone (v. 42) This is a quotation from Psalm 118: 22–23. A corner-stone was one used to bind two walls together. Some corner-stones in the temple in Jerusalem measured 6 metres by 2 metres and were very heavy. Good builders would have recognized the value of such a stone, but this stone – Jesus – had been rejected. The religious leaders saw it as a criticism of themselves.

CHAPTER 22

vv. 1–14 Guests and garments

This is a similar story to Luke 14: 16–24. If it is the same one then it is an interesting example of how the writers use the same material in their own individual ways. The 'dinner party' in Luke becomes a king's son's wedding; the reasons people give for refusing the invitation are different, but the point of the story is the same. God first invited to his 'banquet' the righteous – the religious leaders – but when they would not come, the 'outsiders' took their places.

The invitation To refuse the first call would be serious, to refuse a second time would be a grave insult. But not only did the people refuse – though why they did so is not clear – they resorted to violence and murder. No wonder the king was angry, though his reaction was even more drastic. Perhaps there is a suggestion of symbolism here for the sacking of Jerusalem in A.D. 70, which would still be vividly remembered.

The 'inspection' With the hall full of down-and-outs, many in rags, it seems strange to pick on one not properly dressed. No wonder the poor man was speechless (v. 12). However, the Greek word translated as 'not dressed' (v. 11) indicates a deliberate act: the man did not intend to wear wedding clothes, which was just as much an insult as refusing the invitation. He could have done better but he did not try to. The word given as 'chosen' (v. 14) literally means 'choice', so the sentence reads, 'Many are called, but few are choice' (i.e. worthy).

Some think that this incident is a separate story.

vv. 15–22   The tax trap   (Mark 12: 13–17, Luke 20: 20–26)

It is easy to misunderstand what Jesus meant in his reply to this 'trick question' and to imagine that he left the matter in mid-air. But in fact his answer was clear cut, if a little 'double-edged.'

The tactics The tax was probably the poll tax levied in Syria and Judaea since A.D. 6, and later possibly in Galilee also, which every male Jew had to pay. The point was that the Pharisees, though accepting that the government should be obeyed, put obedience to God first, whilst the Herodians (supporters of Herod Antipas) were more than ready to compromise with Rome. But they both knew how bitterly many Jews resented the tax, so they hoped that Jesus would say either 'Don't pay' – in which case they would have reported him to the Romans as a revolutionary – or 'Yes, pay', in which case they would have told the people he was a supporter of Rome.

The truth Jesus asked for a denarius because it bore the inscription 'Tiberiou Kaisaros' (Emperor Tiberius). He held up the coin to show that since Caesar was Emperor he had to be obeyed, a condition which included the paying of taxes. But man also bore God's image and duty towards Him was greater than to Caesar, in terms of time, talent and allegiance. So Jesus was clarifying the issue for those who thought they could serve both Caesar and God on equal terms.

The irony was that although the Pharisees had set out to trap Jesus, he said what they secretly believed, which was perhaps why they were described as 'hypocrites' (v. 18).

vv. 23–33   One bride, seven brothers   (Mark 12: 18–27, Luke 20: 27–40)

Since the Sadducees did not believe in a resurrection the question was probably not genuine but rather an attempt to get Jesus either to disagree with the Law or to agree that there was no resurrection.

This particular law was given in Deuteronomy 25: 5–6; it stated that if two brothers lived in the same property and one died without leaving a son, then the remaining brother should marry the dead man's wife to ensure that the family line was continued and also to give emotional support to the widow. By the time of Jesus the practice was not popular and the question was not very topical, but the Sadducees thought they could use it to trick Jesus. As it turned out, they had a shock, because Jesus used the question both to show that they did not understand the Scriptures and to shatter some popular ideas about life after death. Resurrection would be a new kind of creation, a new kind of existence.

vv. 34–40 The most important commandment (Mark 12: 28–34, Luke 10: 25–28)

The searcher Mark says that 'one of the lawyers' asked this question, but Matthew says that it was asked after consultation with the Pharisees. A lawyer, also known as a scribe, was a copier of the Law and regarded as an expert in such matters. Perhaps this one wanted Jesus to side with certain schools of thought as to the importance of particular parts of the Law.

The summary There are a number of instances of religious demands being summarized in the Bible. It was sometimes said that Moses had given 613 commandments altogether, that Isaiah (33: 15) reduced them to six and Micah (6: 8) to three. Here, Jesus condenses them to two, with a combination of Deuteronomy 6: 5 and Leviticus 19: 18. It was not only a summary, it was the 'Shema', the central part of a religious creed. If one loves God and one's neighbour, the rest of the commandments fall into place. There is then no desire to kill or steal or harm other people and 'doing good' becomes a delight, not a duty.

vv. 41–46 Greater than David (Mark 12: 35–37, Luke 20: 41–44)

As a climax to these controversies and questions, Matthew records that Jesus asked *them* a question. By anticipating his readers' questions, Matthew makes the matter clearer than Mark does, which is one of the reasons why the early Christians liked this gospel so much. The writer clarifies many of the issues which Mark leaves unexplained.

If they thought of the Messiah as a descendant of the line of David why did David call him 'Lord' (Psalm 110: 1)? It was a question to which they had no answer.

Doesn't this contradict Matthew's 'family tree' in Chapter 1? The word 'descendant' here is intended to mean inferior, rather than a descendant by birth, but it still fits in with Matthew's idea that although Jesus was a descendant of David, he was far greater.

CHAPTER 23   CRITICISMS AND CONDEMNATIONS

This chapter is generally regarded as a 'difficult' one and for good reason. It is a collection of very virulent comments on the Pharisees and it is not easy to accept that all the 'woes' were the words of Jesus. It might be suspected that Jesus's original comments were added to, as later division and bitterness increased between various sects, and that criticisms aimed at other groups were now applied to the Pharisees.

What grounds are there for saying that?
There are two main reasons:
1. Such sweeping denunciations of whole groups were foreign to Jesus's teaching on tolerance and his advice to 'judge not' (7: 1). He knew that there were hypocrites in every group but he would not condemn the whole for the few.
2. It is a 'judgement without justice' in the sense that it contains only criticism and no credit, which is unbalanced and unlike Jesus. Moreover, some of the language (such as vv. 29–36) is a kind of 'verbal violence' that it is impossible to imagine Jesus using.

vv. 1–12   Pretence and practice
Here, the Pharisees in particular are singled out for failing to practise what they preach. They told other people what to do, but did little to help them do it. They loaded the Law on to other people's backs but did not ease the burden by giving a good example. There was far more show than sincerity.

The phylacteries (v. 5)   were small leather boxes which were worn on the arm and on the forehead. The word in classical Greek literally meant 'fortification' and some may have regarded them as a protection against evil. The Hebrew name for them is 'tefillin', which comes from the word for 'prayer'. Inside were strips of vellum on which were written texts from Deuteronomy 6: 8–9 and Exodus 13: 9, but because someone possessed them did not always mean that he practised what was written on them. Some revelled in being called 'teacher' and some had even taken the title 'Father', but they were reminded that God was their Father and Jesus their teacher.

vv. 13–36   The seven woes
The tempo of criticism increases in this focus on the lawyers and Pharisees. Luke gives six woes, Matthew gives seven – a number he uses frequently – and expands them considerably.

It is a catalogue of 'crimes' committed in the name of religion. In the first (v. 13), they are accused of shutting the door of the Kingdom by bad example, instead of opening it. In the second (v. 15), they are accused of persuading someone to become a proselyte (a convert) then making him much worse than he was as a pagan. In the third (v. 16), they are referred to as 'blind guides' because they tell people that only certain oaths made by the altar in the temple are valid, but in fact all oaths are valid if taken in God's name.

The fourth woe (v. 23) tells of the tithes (a tithe is a tenth part) not only on the goods specified in Deuteronomy 14: 22–23, but also on additional items. The lawyers and Pharisees were most meticulous in such observances, but far more important things were neglected. In the attention to detail, a 'gnat' was not allowed through the straining net, but a 'camel', meaning a greater pollution, slipped by unnoticed.

Cups were carefully cleaned on the outside (v. 25) but the inside was filthy. What was the use of fine robes if the mind was unclean? Tombs were whitewashed (v. 27) so that people could see them and avoid 'pollution' by stepping on them. But whitewashing could not disguise what was really inside them.

The last woe (v. 29) criticizes the practice of praising dead prophets but rejecting live ones. If these lawyers and Pharisees had lived at the same time as the prophets would they have been so keen to support them? Their declaration that they would not have taken part in the killing proved that their fathers *had* murdered the prophets.

In the final tirade (v. 33) the writer becomes so carried away that he also gets confused! We know that Cain killed Abel, but the Zechariah who was murdered in the temple (2 Chronicles 24: 21) was the son of Jehoiada. Matthew could mean Zechariah son of Baris, but he was killed in the temple during the attack on Jerusalem in A.D. 70, in which case these could not be the words of Jesus.

vv. 37–39   The last lament

This is a lament of love and seems much more likely to be the genuine words of Jesus. The pleading and the preaching had had little effect and there is a deeply felt sadness in the words. Jesus loved Jerusalem dearly and longed for it to come under the shadow of God's wings (Psalm 57: 1), but the temple no longer contained true worship and the people themselves would reject Jesus.

CHAPTERS 24 AND 25   WAITING AND WATCHING

These two chapters are the 'teaching block' of Matthew's fifth section and they deal with a subject much in the minds of early Christians – last things and last days. They believed that Jesus would return, but they also believed that, since God was the Creator of the world, which man's evil had subsequently spoilt, He would bring the age to an end and then cause there to be a time of peace and goodness. Not surprisingly, these ideas became mingled together and mixed with some very drastic notions about how the world would end, similar to some of the prophecies in the book of Daniel, written during the second century B.C.

Jerusalem from the Mount of Olives

CHAPTER 24   THE END OF THE AGE   (Mark 13, Luke 21)

This chapter is about what is called the Apocalypse, from a Greek word meaning 'to reveal'. It refers to the revelations of the end of Jerusalem and of the world as it was then known. The main point, however, about this end of the world idea was missed (and still is!) by many people. The importance was not so much that mankind would be destroyed, but that God and goodness would triumph over evil.

But isn't the possibility of destruction today very strong?   Yes. For the first time in the world's history, as far as we know, man has the means to destroy life on the earth. He has forgotten that he is not the owner but only the trustee of the world, as the Genesis Creation parables so powerfully show. There is crisis and crime on an unprecedented scale, terrifying exploitation of the earth's resources and a dreadful disregard of human rights and dignity. Add all that together and the mixture is undoubtedly dangerous, but we must also bear in mind that human nature can change for the better and that God's plan for this world must surely be for its deliverance, not its destruction.

vv. 1–2   The temple's end

This was the third temple on this site. It was begun by Herod the Great in 20 B.C. but it was destroyed in A.D. 70, only a few years after it was finished. According to Josephus, the front was covered with great sheets of gold which 'at sunrise reflected a fiery splendour'. But such splendour was doomed.

vv. 3–14 'When will this happen?'

After the introduction to this disaster theme, Matthew raises the obvious question as to when it would happen. The answer seems to be a mixture of the real words of Jesus and a 'reading back' seen from later years and subsequent persecutions. Such terrible events as Jesus predicted can, of course, happen many times in human history, but at such times, many people have found that faith in God sustains them. Whether or not such experiences have been the 'birth pangs of a new age' (v. 8) is another matter. Perhaps they are in the sense that often, after such horrors, nations show a determination that such things shall not happen again.

vv. 15–22 Desperate days

The 'abomination of desolation' comes from Daniel 11: 31. There it referred to the setting up in the temple of a statue of Zeus, the Greek god, by Antiochus Epiphanes in 168 B.C., followed by a sacrifice of pigs on the altar, but here it might refer to the desecration of the temple by the Roman general Titus when he sacked Jerusalem. Such an event was a prelude to very great suffering and distress.

vv. 23–35 False alarms

The Greek word used to describe the return of Jesus to the earth was 'parousia', which meant 'arrival'. Another word sometimes used in this connection is 'eschatology', from the Greek 'eschatos', meaning 'last', though this word was more often used in connection with death and judgement and an after-life.

Despite these warnings the parousia *was* coming though at the time when Matthew was writing many wondered why it should have been delayed. There would be imposters and imitators, but the genuine Messiah would be obvious to all who were really observant, though it is hard to imagine that the 'flashing and lightning' (v. 27) could be missed! It would all be very startling with spectacular signs and dramatic displays, but it might be wondered, bearing in mind that the first visitation took place in a back street in Bethlehem, whether a second coming would be quite so conspicuous as the writers believed!

The phrase 'present generation' (v. 34) indicates how certain they were of this return.

Many Christians today still wait for this second coming, but others believe that the experience at Pentecost (Acts 2) was the return of Jesus in the form of the Holy Spirit, when his 'body' became the Church.

vv. 36–44 No one knows when

The difference between v. 34 and v. 36 is strange and they appear to give opposite ideas. The most important point, however, is to be prepared for whenever it might happen. No doubt in Noah's day many sceptics laughed

96

at his labours and at his 'foolish ideas' about the flood, but they must later have regretted their ridicule.

vv. 45–51   Faithful and foolish servants   (Luke 12: 41–48)
Matthew drives home the point about being prepared by following it with a parable about two servants, one faithful, the other feckless. One worked as though his master was there, but to the other the master was 'out of sight, out of mind'. The meaning is clear: the demand to do God's work can come at any time; in the meantime, there must be a sense of responsibility and a willingness to work.

'Cut him to pieces' (v. 51) is sometimes changed to 'throw him out' or 'punish him'.

CHAPTER 25   PARABLES ON RESPONSIBILITY

Some refer to this as a chapter on future judgement, but it seems to me to deal more with present conduct rather than with people's fate in the future. The three stories appear to deal with that same theme.

vv. 1–13   The wedding
The odd thing about this parable is that, though there is reference to the bridegroom and the bridesmaids, there is no mention of the bride. I suppose, since the bridegroom was on his way to claim her, she does not really come into the story. Additionally, and perhaps more pertinently, if the early Church saw Jesus as the bridegroom, it would not be easy to fit the bride into the allegory (though some regard the Church as the bride).

The occasion   A wedding was a great event in Galilee, with the guests excused any religious duties so that they might attend, and even the study of the Law was suspended. Apparently, a wedding was considered more important than studying the Scriptures! The high point of the proceedings came when the groom went to the bride's home and then took her to their new home, probably in some kind of conveyance, with the bridesmaids escorting her. The entire wedding proceedings could last several days and on at least one occasion Jesus was invited to the ceremony (John 2: 1–11).

The attendants   To have ten girls as attendants was not unusual, neither was the fact that the groom did not come until midnight. They were not tied to time as we are today. But what was strange was that, although they were all expecting him and presumably eager to play their part, only half of the girls were really ready. They had been conscientious while the others had been careless, although the latter could be excused for thinking that perhaps their lamps would not be needed. The refusal to help sounds selfish, but perhaps there was not time to share the oil and to wash afterwards. (It might also be asked where they would find a shop open at midnight!) The point was that when they finally lit their lamps they were too late.

Oil lamp of the type used in New Testament times

The object   This parable can certainly be allegorized in the sense that it can refer to the second coming, with Jesus as the bridegroom. The girls could represent those who were waiting for the coming and wondering why it was delayed; they could also be the people who had grown tired of waiting.

But I believe the emphasis is as much on the readiness as on the return. Preparedness is an individual responsibility. The opportunity to co-operate with Christ may occur at any time, as the Good Samaritan found (Luke 10: 25). A Christian who thinks that God can be met only 'by appointment' at church on a Sunday is mistaken.

vv. 14–30   The wealth   (Luke 19: 11–27)

The original translation had the word 'talents' because a talent was an amount of money, either of gold or silver. Estimating its value in modern money is not easy, because a talent could vary in weight; this is why modern versions say 'bags of gold' or 'talents of money'. However, whatever value we put on a talent, the truth seems clear:

1. The number of talents varied, but the opportunity was the same and the responsibility was in proportion. There are many more one- and two-talent people than five-talent people in the world but that does not mean that less is expected from them.

2. The talents were not gifts, they were trusts and were given to each man 'according to his abilities'. The time came when each had to account for the trust that had been placed in him.

3. The servants represented their master while he was away. He had left them to carry on his business and to use the money for *his* enrichment, not their own.

4. Increasing the value no doubt entailed risk, but it was the one who had buried his talent who was blamed. He accused his master of injustice, but the real reason for his failure was his own fear and lack of faith.

5. It is easy to say that the parable was aimed at the religious leaders, who had been entrusted with the 'treasures' of the Scriptures and had 'buried' them, but it is also true of many other precious things in life.

So once again we have a parable about being prepared to serve God with whatever talents are possessed.

vv. 31–46   The well-doing

This tremendous climax to the fifth section and to the series of sayings of Jesus is not only peculiar to Matthew but is more like an illustration of perfection than a parable. It is a superb example of the very best in Jewish and Christian ethics. It has been called the most clear-cut parable on judgement. The 'heavenly' verdict is on what has been done on earth.

The sheep and goats   It was a typical Palestinian scene, with the sheep a lighter colour than the goats. The two did not mix, so they were used as a symbol of separation. The 'right hand' so often in the Bible represented a place of honour. (The fact that even today in some countries left-handed people are distrusted may be related to this.)

The surprises   This is a gospel of the King and the Kingdom, and this last parable is about the King on his throne. However, the heavenly scene has some very down-to-earth implications:
1. The usual way of forming judgement was to ask whether a person had kept the Law faithfully, but Jesus put the test on to a different plane. They were asked not about whether they had kept the Law, or worshipped regularly, only about what they had done for one another.
2. The ones who were praised had no idea that their goodness had even been noticed, let alone that it merited any kind of reward. It had evidently not been done to gain any kind of credit.
3. The uncaring were not so much callous as careless, in not seeing the connection between concern for the needy and religious belief. Surely, allegiance to the King and showing concern for beggars were two different things? But they were not. The King was involved in the suffering of his subjects.

Is this the most important part of religion?   It has always been seen as essential, but I think one has to be careful that it doesn't become a substitute for a relationship with God. Helping the needy cannot guarantee a good relationship with God, but a good relationship with God can guarantee that a person will want to help the needy. In the early Church, as we see in the Acts of the Apostles, the Church leaders collected money for famine relief, but I am sure that Paul would have said that such concern was a by-product of his faith. As guidance for a true relationship with God, I feel he would have referred to his Letters to the Romans and the Corinthians. Faith without good works may be dead, but good works without faith could be just as empty.

CHAPTERS 26–28   THE FINAL DRAMA

After his final summary of the teaching section (26: 1), the writer now moves on to the climax of this and all the gospels – the Last Supper, the trials, death and resurrection of Jesus. This section was almost certainly the first part to have a fixed form of narrative and to be written down, but in such a story variations and additions are to be expected since it is written from different experiences and memories.

CHAPTER 26

vv. 2–5   The plot   (Mark 14: 1–2, Luke 22: 1–2)

All the gospels agree that Jesus was crucified on a Friday, so this plotting must have taken place on the Wednesday. Mark seems to be combining the Passover with the Feast of Unleavened Bread (though strictly they were not the same), but Matthew, always wanting to get things clear, refers only to 'the Passover'. The word comes from the Hebrew 'pesah', meaning 'to spare'; the Greek word 'Paskha' meant the same. The festival commemorated the fact that the Angel of Death passed over the Israelites and spared them when they were in Egypt (Exodus 12), before the Exodus began.

Mark is rather vague as to who organized this plot against Jesus, but Matthew has no doubt it was Joseph Caiaphas, who was High Priest from A.D. 18 to A.D. 36.

vv. 6–13   The trust   (Mark 14: 3–9)

All the gospels tell of a woman who anointed Jesus with precious ointment, but Luke (7: 36–50) and John (12: 1–8) appear to be referring to a different occasion. However, there seems little doubt that this woman, whoever she was, wanted to show that she believed Jesus to be the Messiah, the 'anointed one'. Why exactly she came in at this time is not clear, but her motives were misunderstood by the disciples, who thought it a mere waste of money. Jesus, however, saw it as an anointing for burial, not Messiahship.

vv. 14–16   The treachery   (Mark 14: 10–11, Luke 22: 3–6)

Why Judas acted as he did has been the subject of controversy ever since, but it seems likely that he was motivated by political purposes rather than by money. Thirty pieces of silver were the amount fixed in Exodus 21: 32 as compensation for the death of a slave. The words in v. 15 are taken directly from Zechariah 11: 12, which raises the question of whether Matthew is 'finding' yet another prophecy to fit his purpose.

If Judas was a nationalist who was longing to see Israel delivered from the enemy, he may well have thought that if Jesus was arrested, his supporters would stage a rescue and start some kind of revolution, or even that Jesus himself might effect a miraculous deliverance and show everyone that he was the Messiah. But the question still remains, 'Just what exactly did Judas betray?' Nothing was said at the trials about his 'evidence', so it seems that probably he betrayed only the place where Jesus might be found.

vv. 17–30   The farewell meal   (Mark 14: 12–21, Luke 22: 7–30, John 13)

The arguments as to whether the meal was actually the Passover meal or not are complex. To summarize, all the gospels agree that the supper took place on the evening before the crucifixion, i.e. on the Thursday, but while the synoptics say that it was the Passover meal, John's gospel says that the Passover did not begin until the evening of the Friday, therefore the Last Supper could not have been the meal eaten at the beginning of Passover. There are points in favour of both views, but many scholars think that if the Last Supper was not the actual Passover meal, then it was probably a 'fellowship' meal, called 'kiddush', shared privately by families or groups of friends, often at the beginning of a festival. A blessing would be said over a cup of wine at the beginning of the meal.

It certainly seems that the arrangements for the supper were carefully made, though Matthew does not mention the man with the water jar referred to by both Mark and Luke, and, perhaps more strangely, he does not say that one of the two disciples was Peter (Luke 22: 8). There is a tradition that it was the house of John Mark's mother, Mary (Acts 12).

The supper   This meal is commemorated by many Christians by the 'Eucharist', from the Greek word meaning 'thanksgiving'. It is the most solemn sacrament of the Christian Church, though it is known by different names in different denominations and is celebrated more frequently in some Churches than in others. The gospels are not the earliest record of what took place at this meal: Paul described it when he wrote to the Christians at Corinth, in about A.D. 52 (1 Corinthians 11).

Just as the father, or host, does at a Jewish meal, Jesus took the bread, blessed it, broke it – it was flat unleavened bread – then handed it round. The usual words were, 'Blessed art thou, O Lord, who brings forth bread from the earth.' But this breaking of the bread had a new meaning. Jesus's body was going to be broken, but his death would be as bread is to the body – a benefit and a blessing.

The cup may have been made of metal or possibly of wood. By tradition it has come to be known as the 'Holy Grail' and was later supposed to have been brought to Glastonbury in England by Joseph of Arimathea. At the Last Supper it represented the 'covenant' referred to in Exodus 24: 8, when Moses sprinkled the blood of the sacrifice on the people to signify the agreement made with God. It was also a reference to the 'new covenant' of Jeremiah (31: 31). The Greek word translated as 'covenant' could also mean 'testament' or 'agreement'. This is why the Christian Bible is in two parts, representing two agreements with God: the Old Testament, based on the commandment at Sinai, and the New Testament, the agreement with God through the life and death of Jesus.

The shock (v. 23) Since eating together was a sign of friendship, the warning of a betrayer was as shattering as it was sudden. In the other gospels all the disciples wondered whom Jesus meant, in Matthew's account alone does Judas speak (v. 25). Possibly Matthew included this because he saw no reason why Judas should be shielded, though once Judas had been named it could be asked why the other disciples did not try to stop him.

vv. 31–35   The sheep   (Mark 14: 27–31, Luke 22: 31–34)
The quotation is from Zechariah (13: 7), who seems to be a favourite Old Testament prophet for Matthew. Peter's protest is also typical of this gospel. Jesus's rebuke showed that Peter's promise was a rash one, but all the disciples reacted in the same way. The 'cock-crow' may have been the trumpet call to mark the third watch (about 3 a.m.) of the Roman soldiers.

vv. 36–46   The anguish   (Mark 14: 32–42, Luke 22: 39–46)
The Mount of Olives in fact consisted of several hills on the eastern side of Jerusalem. There were olive trees on the lower slopes and the Garden of Gethsemane was an orchard amongst the trees. Today it looks more like a garden in our sense of the word, with flowers and shrubs, but it also has some very ancient olive trees.

This was Jesus's darkest hour: he knew what he had to face, but even worse than the physical pain would be the mental agony of desertion and disbelief. Verse 38 is one of the rare examples in this gospel of Jesus's emotions, as he is overwhelmed with anguish. The 'cup' signifies emotion, here meaning the very depths of suffering, but 'as thou wilt' was not said in despair, it was an avowal of willingness to do whatever God wanted.

vv. 47–56   The arrest   (Mark 14: 43–50, Luke 22: 47–53, John 18: 3–12)
Whether the disciples' failure to keep watch would have made much difference is debatable, for they were heavily outnumbered. A kiss on the cheek was the usual greeting of a disciple to a rabbi. It was a sign of loyalty and respect, but here in the darkness, as a means of identifying the man to arrest, it became a sign of treachery.

v. 50 This quotation of Jesus, found only in Matthew, may be associated with some words found on a very ancient drinking cup, 'Friend, what are you here for?' Jesus may have been reminding Judas of the Last Supper.

In John's gospel (18: 10) Peter is named as using the sword.

The reference in v. 56 may be to Isaiah 53.

What does v. 52 mean? It has often been used to signify whatever particular people want it to mean. Some use it to defend the use of arms, saying that it means that the aggressors deserve to die, while others say that it refers to the futility of trying to resist a far more powerful foe. It certainly means, I think, that in resistance and revenge many precious things perish, whoever wins.

Ancient olive trees in the Garden of Gethsemane

vv. 53–54 These verses look a little like another of Matthew's reflections in which he anticipates the readers' questions. Many of his readers must have wondered whether Jesus *could* have been 'delivered' if God had so decreed it. But then how would the Scriptures – possibly Isaiah 53 and Psalms 22 and 69 – be 'fulfilled'?

The 'twelve legions of angels' are in sharp contrast to the twelve disciples (if we include Judas) who 'forsook him and fled'.

vv. 57–68   The Jewish trial   (Mark 14: 53–65, Luke 22: 63–71)

There is much debate among scholars about the accounts of the Jewish trial of Jesus, particularly in view of the contentions that the trial was not conducted according to Jewish law. However, here we will confine our examination to Matthew's account of this event.

By now it was very late on the Thursday night and this 'trial', which according to Mark and Matthew took place at the house of the High Priest, was largely a farce, for several reasons.

1.   It was unlawful for the Council of the Sanhedrin to meet at night. Even if the Law had been disregarded, it is improbable that they would all have been able to gather in the middle of the night. It was far more likely to have been a meeting only of Caiaphas and a few of his friends, hastily summoned or probably warned in advance to be prepared.

2.   Oral tradition, later written down as the Mishnah, decreed that a trial of this nature should not be held on the eve of a festival or a festival itself and must take place during daylight.

3.   According to Deuteronomy 19: 16–19, a witness giving false evidence should be 'treated as he intended to treat his fellow', but here this law was ignored. The witnesses were not cross-examined, nor are we told that they were reprimanded.

4.   The only form of blasphemy punishable by death was the reviling of God's name (Leviticus 24: 16). Telling the High Priest that he would 'see the Son of Man seated at the right hand of God and coming on the clouds of heaven' could hardly be said to come into that category. This is probably why there was no suggestion or indication that the usual punishment for blasphemy – stoning – was carried out.

Jesus's refusal to answer any of the 'charges' (v. 63) made Caiaphas resort to sharp practice. He got Jesus to convict *himself* by asking him, on oath, whether or not he was the Messiah. This was also unlawful because no one could be convicted on his own testimony. Caiaphas interpreted the reply as evidence of Jesus's guilt and then made a great show of being outraged by the claim (v. 65).

vv. 67–68   The contempt

The condemned man now had no rights and, apparently, no friends! However, it is hardly likely that the whole Council, if they were there, would indulge in such behaviour as striking and spitting on the prisoner. It was probably just a few who would resort to such treatment. Mark says that they blindfolded Jesus, which would explain the taunt, 'tell us who hit you' (v. 68).

vv. 69–75   The cowardice   (Mark 14: 66–72, Luke 22: 54–62, John 18: 25 –27)

Trying to explain Peter's action is not easy. Some even doubt whether it ever really happened, since it could cast grave doubts on Peter's worthiness subsequently to become a leader of the Church. But it seems to me to show that even Peter could fail in his loyalty, yet could be forgiven and become a changed character.

The gospel accounts differ as to who challenged him and what made them suspicious. Matthew says it was his Galilean accent that gave him away. Both Mark and Matthew record Peter's sorrow. The 'big fisherman', as he is sometimes called, behaved like anything but a rock: he broke down and wept like a child.

CHAPTER 27   GOOD FRIDAY

vv. 1–2   Introduction   (Mark 15: 1, Luke 23: 1–2)
Matthew indicates that there was a second meeting of the Sanhedrin. Perhaps they had decided that the 'trial' during the night had been inadequate, and they wanted to make more suitable plans before taking Jesus to Pilate, the Roman Governor.

Pontius Pilate had been appointed Governor or Procurator of Judaea in A.D. 26 by the Emperor Tiberius. He was later removed from office, in A.D. 36, because of excessive cruelty towards his subjects. Josephus tells us that Pilate tried to keep order in a province 'seething with discontent' but that his record was 'very bad', which seems to be putting it mildly! Pilate usually lived at Caesarea, on the coast, but was probably in Jerusalem at this time to keep an eye on the Passover pilgrims who were crowding into the city.

Why was Jesus taken to Pilate?   Certainly not because the Jews had any regard for Pilate or the way he governed. They hated him for all kinds of reasons, not least for the fact that he had brought military standards, bearing Caesar's image, into Jerusalem and these had offended the Jews. They had protested strongly, at which Pilate had threatened a massacre, but in the end he had removed the standards. Another reason, according to Josephus (*Antiquities* XVIII 3: 2), was that he had used 'sacred' temple money to build an aqueduct and in that instance the protest had led to many Jews being murdered.

Here, however, the elders seemed to be using him to get rid of Jesus, because if they could get Jesus convicted by a Roman court the matter would be legal and in the process they would also be taking revenge on Pilate by putting him in a difficult position.

vv. 3–10   Interlude
Matthew and Luke (Acts 1: 18) give different accounts of how Judas died and to try to reconcile them is unwise. Both say that he came to a bad end and that the money was used to buy land, but whereas Matthew says he committed suicide, Luke says he died from some kind of accidental fall.

Personally, I feel a little suspicious of Matthew's version because it seems to be another example of his practice of finding and moulding an Old Testament prophecy to fit his purpose. This time, however, he is confused. It was Zechariah (11: 13), not Jeremiah, who spoke of throwing the silver back into the treasury. In Hebrew there is little difference between the word for 'treasury' and that for 'potter', so, by means of a play on words, Matthew connects this event with Jeremiah's visit to the potter (Jeremiah 18) and with his later purchase of a field (Jeremiah 32).

A further complication is that the Hebrew 'Akeldama' (Acts 1: 19), meaning 'blood acre', as used here (v. 8), could also possibly mean 'field of sleeping', or a cemetery, which would explain v. 7.

What seems certain from Matthew's account is that Judas realized that he had betrayed an innocent man (v. 4).

vv. 11–26   The Roman trial   (Mark 15: 2–15, Luke 23: 3–25, John 18: 28 – 19: 16)

Interrogation (vv. 11–14)   The religious leaders must have realized that their charge against Jesus of blasphemy was very flimsy and would carry no weight whatever with Pilate. So they changed the charge to one of treason, saying that Jesus had claimed to be a king and therefore in opposition to the Roman Emperor. These charges are given more fully in Luke (23: 1–2). Pilate soon seemed to realize that such a charge was ridiculous and was very surprised that Jesus remained silent in the face of the accusation. Most prisoners would have protested their innocence.

Which Jesus? (vv. 15–18)   Though it is mentioned in three of the gospels, there is no other evidence for this so-called custom of releasing a prisoner at Passover.

Some versions of Matthew say that Barabbas was also named Jesus, which would not have been unusual, but it does raise the question as to whether the crowd knew exactly which man they were shouting for and whether all the tumult in favour of the terrorist was as clear-cut as it appeared. It could have been that it was a well-organized section of pro-Barabbas supporters who swayed the crowd, or perhaps it was some of the men who had been present at the Feeding of the Five Thousand, when Jesus had turned down the job as leader (John 6: 15), so now they turned to the terrorist. Matthew, however, says that the real reason for Jesus being taken to Pilate was jealousy (v. 18).

Interruption (v. 19)   Only Matthew tells of the plea from Pilate's wife on behalf of an 'innocent man'. Some people regard this as an example of real concern, others dismiss it as mere superstition, but the Orthodox Church has been determined to think the best of her and has made her a saint. Tradition says that her name was Claudia Procula.

Although Pilate was not apparently influenced by his wife's message, he was in a difficult dilemma. He probably knew that the charges against Jesus were false. He knew too that Emperor Tiberius was very harsh on governors who did not maintain law and order, and that anyone suspected of treason had to be dealt with severely. The gospels differ in their accounts of how Pilate reacted to this dilemma. Luke and John say that he tried hard to get Jesus freed, Mark and Matthew indicate that he was indifferent and unwilling, or even unable, to see that justice was done. Matthew has no doubt that he backed down in the face of mob violence.

The hand-washing (v. 24) Only Matthew mentions this incident. It must be confessed that it is hard to imagine that a Roman governor, especially one with Pilate's reputation for ruthlessness, would have made such a public gesture of indecision and weakness. Surely the Emperor would have wanted to know why Pilate had so obviously opted out of his responsibilities. He would want to know why, if the prisoner was innocent, he was not freed, and if he was guilty, he was not given a fair trial.

It is also unlikely, in my view, that 'all the people' wanted 'his blood to be on us and on our children' (v. 25). This verse sounds very much like a product of later anti-Jewish attitudes.

Who was to blame? There has been a great deal of debate over this question. Jews do not accept the traditional view that the death of Jesus was instigated by the Jewish religious leaders and carried out by the Romans. But the historical issue is not the end of it. The crucifixion is contemporary: by that I mean that the actions and attitudes of Pilate, Peter, Caiaphas and the crowd all represent elements of human nature which are always present in the world and which combine to crucify Christ, in the sense that hypocrisy, greed, envy, love of violence, etc., put to death things that are good. We can all think of examples of when people have preferred violence to peace, Barabbas rather than Christ.

vv. 27–31   The insults   (Mark 15: 16–20, John 19: 2–3)
Pilate's 'palace' was the praetorium, his headquarters when he was in Jerusalem. Matthew says that 'the whole company' of soldiers took part in this second assault on Jesus, but a battalion was six hundred men, so it might be asked why, if there were that many soldiers present, they had apparently been unable to control the crowd.

The mockery was centred on the title 'king', hence the scarlet robe, the 'crown' of thorns, the 'sceptre' in his hand, and the greeting 'Hail, King of the Jews', which was also a satire on the Roman phrase 'Hail, Caesar'. The whole purpose was to pour contempt on what they alleged was Jesus's claim to be a king.

vv. 32–44   The crucifixion   (Mark 15: 21–32, Luke 23: 26–43, John 19: 17 –27)
Crucifixion was a dreadful form of capital punishment, reserved for rebels and criminals of the worst type and never used for a Roman citizen. The

victim was first flogged then forced to carry the cross-beam – the 'patibulum' – tied across his back through the streets and out to the place of execution.

The gospels call this place 'Golgotha', from the Aramaic word 'galgatha', meaning 'skull'. Whether this was because it was shaped like a skull or whether it was because it was a place of death is not certain. Sometimes it is known as 'Calvary', from the Latin word for skull, 'calvaria'.

Once the site was reached, the cross-beam was bolted to the upright piece, the victim fastened to it (either by nails or bound with ropes), the whole thing lifted up and dropped into a socket in the ground, and the person just left to die. Sometimes, to make the agony worse, the victim was fastened to the cross in an awkward position. It usually took a long time to die by crucifixion.

Matthew mentions Simon (v. 32), who was forced to carry the cross-beam when Jesus collapsed, but does not mention his sons, as Mark does. He also tells us that someone offered Jesus a drug to deaden the pain, but that Jesus refused it. The drug was 'gall', a bitter and possibly poisonous herb called in Hebrew 'rosh'; probably Matthew had Psalm 69: 21 in mind, where the translation is 'vinegar'.

The gambling (v. 35) The four soldiers who had carried out the execution were entitled to whatever the victim possessed as a kind of 'reward' for their brutal duty. This verse is also a fulfilment of the words in Psalm 22: 18.

The charge (v. 37) The inscription, or 'titulus', stated the nature of the crime committed by the crucified person. It was often nailed to the cross, above the victim's head, or sometimes hung round his neck. Jesus's 'crime' was that he had claimed to be a king.

The criminals (v. 38) The fact that he was put to death with convicted criminals showed that Jesus was regarded as being in the same category. Tradition has given the other two victims names – Dysmas and Gestas – and Luke (23: 40) indicates that one of them repented before he died.

The abuse (vv. 39–44) This is the third instance of mockery and three groups take part in it this time: the passers-by, who had apparently come from a nearby road to see what was going on and to join in the jeering, the priests and, finally, the two criminals. In fact, the words 'he saved others', though intended to be mocking, were true. He *had* saved others: that was what he had come into the world to do (1: 21). But the invitation to 'save himself' (v. 42) would have meant using his powers to 'prove' his Messiahship, which was what the first temptation had been about (4: 2).

vv. 45–56 The death of Jesus (Mark 15: 33–41, Luke 23: 44–49, John, 19: 28–30)

The mention of darkness falling at midday (v. 45) is Matthew's first indication of the time of day, but all the synoptic gospels agree that Jesus died at three o'clock in the afternoon. The darkness may have been caused by a storm, or even by an eclipse of the sun, which is calculated to have happened at that time. It is more likely, however, that Matthew regards the darkness as a sign of disaster, as in Isaiah 60: 2.

Despair? (v. 46)   This quotation from Psalm 22: 1 is sometimes seen as a cry of despair and the words pose some problems. Matthew gives the Hebrew 'Eli', not Mark's Aramaic 'Eloi', but few Jews would have mistaken 'Eli' for 'Elijah', though, of course, the words may not have been clear. Psalm 22 starts on a note of despair, but then moves on to a tone of triumph, and there are some remarkable parallels between that Psalm and the death of Jesus. However, it has to be acknowledged that in such a moment of extreme agony Jesus may have wondered, with the psalmist, whether God *had* 'forsaken' him.

The death (v. 50)   This seemed to happen comparatively quickly. Some crucifixion victims took several days to die. The 'loud cry' may have been the last line of Psalm 22 – 'All this the Lord has done' – which is certainly not a cry of despair.

The 'curtain' in the temple formed a barrier between the Holy of Holies (which only the priests could enter) and the Holy Place. Josephus says there were two curtains, each about 18 metres high and 'woven with great richness'. The phenomenon of the curtain being torn in two was symbolic. The curtain had been the barrier between the priests, who were set apart, and the ordinary people. By the death of Jesus, this 'barrier' had been removed and the way to God became more accessible to everyone.

The 'opening of the graves' (vv. 52–53) is found only in Matthew and is often seen as a foreshadowing of the resurrection. It could have been associated with an earth tremor which, in that part of the world, would not be uncommon.

The verdict (v. 54)   The gospels vary a little as to what the centurion actually said. He is mentioned in all three synoptics: according to Mark and Matthew he called Jesus 'a son of God', but Luke says he referred to Jesus as 'innocent'. By tradition, he has been given various names, such as Longinnus and Petronius.

vv. 57–61   The burial   (Mark 15: 42–47, Luke 23: 50–56, John 19: 38–42)
The 'women who watched' are contrasted sharply with the disciples who deserted!

Mary, from the village of Magdala, is mentioned a number of times in the gospels, but suffers from what is almost certainly an unfounded reputation. Luke says (8: 2) that Jesus cured her of 'seven devils', which has led some to suppose that she was an immoral woman, but it is more likely that she was cured of some form of mental illness, not moral weakness.

Mary, mother of James and Joseph, is not easy to identify. Some believe that she was a relative of Jesus's mother and some have even suggested that she may have been the wife of Cleopas (Cleopas is mentioned in Luke 24: 13).

The mother of James and John is presumably Salome, if Mark (15: 41) is referring to the same woman.

Joseph was from the village of Arimathaea; this may be the same place as Ramah, mentioned in 1 Samuel 1: 1.

Mark says that Joseph was a member of the Sanhedrin, whilst the other gospels say he was a disciple of Jesus, though a 'secret' one. Matthew takes Mark's word 'respected' to mean 'rich', which Joseph probably was. He was also a brave man, because to ask Pilate for the body of a crucified man might well have aroused suspicion that he was associated with the criminal.

Moreover, to offer his family tomb for the burial was a considerable sacrifice, since many rabbis forbade the use of a tomb for future family burials if it had contained the body of a condemned man. Perhaps Joseph was doing all this out of kindness, though he might also have been anxious to make up for his apparent failure to speak out in Jesus's favour at the Jewish trial.

The Law The Romans were not concerned about a body remaining on a cross – in fact, it served as a warning to other would-be criminals – but the Jewish Law (Deuteronomy 21: 23) stated that a body should not remain on a 'gibbet' overnight. Since burials could not take place on the Sabbath, it was important to remove the body before the Sabbath began that evening.

v. 61 Matthew emphasizes that the women who watched noted carefully where the body was laid, because one later 'explanation' of the resurrection was that the women went to the *wrong* tomb on the Sunday morning.

vv. 62–66 Sealed and secured

This story is found only in Matthew among the New Testament gospels, though it is also found in the apocryphal 'Gospel of Peter'. It is obviously used by Matthew to show that the body was not stolen, that idea being another of the later attempts to 'explain' the resurrection. But if it is claimed that someone stole the body, then it must also be explained who was supposed to have stolen it and why it was not produced to prove that the resurrection was not true. If the disciples were supposed to have taken it in order to 'prove' the resurrection, why were they later willing to suffer and die for something which, in that case, they would have known was not true?

This is the last we hear of Pilate in the gospels. We know that he was recalled to Rome in A.D. 36, after a massacre of some Samaritans at Mount Gerizim, but after that facts are few and legends are plentiful. Some say he was executed and some that he committed suicide. It has even been declared that he became a martyr and the Coptic Church (the Egyptian Christian Church) remembers him as such in June each year.

At the end of Anatole France's fictional work *The Procurator of Judaea* are the words, 'Pilate contracted his brows ... in the attitude of one who probes the deeps of memory. Then, after a silence of some seconds: "Jesus?" he murmured, "Jesus – of Nazareth? I cannot call him to mind."' But the truth is that it is Pilate who would never have been recalled to mind, had he not presided over the trial of Jesus.

CHAPTER 28   THE RESURRECTION   (Mark 16, Luke 24, John 20–21)

Matthew, fine artist that he is, paints a vivid picture of what happened on the Sunday morning – the 'third day', since the Friday is counted as the first day. The resurrection is the foundation of the Christian faith and the reason for the writing of the gospels. There are many aspects of it which are quite outside the scope of scientific or historical investigation, but despite the kind of differences which one would expect in such a drama, the fact remains that many people were completely convinced that they had seen Jesus alive after his death.

Furthermore, these appearances occurred at different times and in different places, usually to more than one person. These eyewitnesses did not attempt to explain their experiences, they simply described what they had seen and heard, from their own point of view. They were more concerned with the delight of it all than with the exact agreement of details.

vv. 1–10   The wonder

It is to be assumed that the 'other Mary' is the same as the one in 27: 56. According to Mark, the three women who were at the cross had come to embalm the body with spices, as was the Jewish custom. Matthew refers to only two women and simply says that they had come to 'look at' the tomb, possibly to try to decide how they were going to get into a tomb which had a sealed entrance and a guard of four Roman soldiers.

Matthew has his own ideas as to how the heavy round stone was rolled back from the entrance. He says that an angel moved the stone, though he seems to have been helped by an earth tremor (28: 2)! The sudden appearance of the angel also explains the helplessness of the guards. But the real reason for the 'messenger' (which is what the word 'angelos' means) being there was to tell the terrified women that Jesus had been raised from death and would meet the disciples in Galilee.

The bowing down   The women's first reaction was a mixture of fear and joy, followed by a decision to go and do something about the message by telling the disciples as quickly as possible. On the way, according to this gospel, they were confronted by Jesus and it is interesting to notice that in this, as in every other appearance, there is a marked change of attitude on the part of those who saw him. Previously they had regarded him as a

111

prophet or a teacher, but now they 'worshipped' him. There was obviously some quality about him that they had never noticed before.

vv. 11–15 The bribery
This is another incident found only in Matthew. It is one which raises difficulties, because for Roman soldiers to admit that they had been asleep on duty would have meant drastic punishment and probably death. Matthew does not elaborate on that point, however; his purpose is to show that the idea of the disciples stealing the body was fiction, not fact, and that the story originated with a case of bribery.

vv. 16–20 The blessing   (Mark 16: 14–18)
It is interesting to see how each gospel ends. Mark ends abruptly and unfinished, as far as the most genuine manuscripts are concerned (this is discussed in the commentary on that gospel). Luke ends with the disciples going back from Bethany to Jerusalem to await further instructions for their work as witnesses. John concludes – for most scholars believe that 20: 31 is the end of that gospel – with the hope that the reader may have 'eternal life' through the belief that Jesus is the Son of God.

Matthew's gospel comes to its conclusion and climax with the risen Christ meeting the disciples in Galilee, where the ministry began and where it is now going to end, with Jesus giving them their final commission and final promise.

The place 'The mountain' may have been a particular one, perhaps where they had met before, or even where Jesus had given the Sermon on the Mount, but it is more likely to be Matthew's way of making it a 'mountain-top' experience, like so many of the Old Testament revelations of God.

The people The eleven disciples are mentioned, though there may have been more people present. While some seemed wary of accepting the resurrection, the rest 'worshipped'. To me, this doubting by some of the disciples shows the honesty of the story. If it had been presented as a 'perfect ending' with no indication that anyone was reluctant to believe it, it would have seemed less credible. As it is, it represents the whole reaction to the resurrection: some doubted, the rest saw a different Jesus.

The purpose The reason for gathering the disciples together in Galilee was to give them final instructions and assurance. They were to go out into the world – to Jew and gentile – to preach, teach and baptize, a practice which became the usual method of gaining converts to the Church. The Greek world literally means baptize 'into the name of' and the phrase originally meant the giving to someone of a precious object for protection and safe keeping. Thus, the expression here conveys the idea of entrusting someone's most precious possession – life itself – into God's keeping and care.

112

The promise Matthew ends his account on a mountain, with a tremendous promise, not only to those who were present, but by implication to all followers, that Christ would be with them till the 'end of time'. This is a better translation than 'the end of the world', which perhaps arose from the early Christian idea that the world would shortly come to an end. Matthew began his gospel by saying that Jesus would be called 'Emmanuel', meaning 'God with us' (1: 23). Now he ends by showing that 'God with us' was not only Jesus's name, but also described his nature.

Moonrise over the Valley of the Cross, Jerusalem

Appendix

Incident	Matthew	Mark	Luke
Jesus's family tree	1: 1–17		3: 23–28
The birth of Jesus	1: 18–25		2: 1–20
The visitors from the East	2: 1–12		
The escape to Egypt	2: 13–15		
The killing of the children	2: 16–18		
The return from Egypt	2: 19–23		
The appearance and preaching of John	3: 1–12	1: 1–8	3: 1–20
The baptism of Jesus	3: 13–17	1: 9–11	3: 21–22
The temptations in the wilderness	4: 1–11	1: 12–13	4: 1–13
The mission begins	4: 12–17	1: 14–15	4: 14–15
The call of the first disciples	4: 18–22	1: 16–20	5: 1–11
Preaching and healing	4: 23–25	1: 39	6: 17–19
The sermon on the hill			
The Beatitudes	5: 1–12		6: 20–23
Salt and light	5: 13–16	9: 50	14: 34–35
The importance of the Law	5: 17–20		
Anger	5: 21–26		
Adultery	5: 27–30		
Divorce	5: 31–32	10: 11–12	16: 18
Vows	5: 33–37		
Revenge	5: 38–42		6: 27–31
Love for enemies	5: 43–48		6: 32–36
Giving to charity	6: 1–4		
Praying	6: 5–15		11: 2–4
Fasting	6: 16–18		
True treasures	6: 19–21		12: 33–34
The light of the body	6: 22–23		11: 34–36
Unnecessary worrying	6: 24–34		12: 22–31
Judging others	7: 1–6		6: 37–42
Asking and knocking	7: 7–12		11: 9–13
The narrow gate	7: 13–14		13: 24
False prophets	7: 15–20		6: 43–44
False followers	7: 21–23		13: 25–27
The two houses	7: 24–27		6: 47–49
The people's amazement	7: 28–29		
Healing a leper	8: 1–4	1: 40–45	5: 12–16
Healing the centurion's servant	8: 5–13		7: 1–10
Healing Peter's mother-in-law	8: 14–17	1: 29–31	4: 38–39
The would-be disciples	8: 18–22		9: 57–62
Calming the tempest	8: 23–27	4: 35–41	8: 22–25

Incident	Matthew	Mark	Luke
Tombs and torments	8: 28–34	5: 1–20	8: 26–39
The faithful friends	9: 1–8	2: 1–12	5: 17–26
The calling of Matthew	9: 9–13	2: 13–17	5: 27–32
Fasting and patching	9: 14–17	2:18–22	5: 33–39
The daughter who died and the woman with haemorrhages	9: 18–26	5: 21–43	8: 40–56
Healing the blind men	9: 27–31	(8: 22–26 similar)	
Healing the dumb man	9: 32–34	(7: 32 similar)	(11: 14 similar)
Pity for the people	9: 35–38	6: 34	10: 2
Choosing the Twelve	10: 1–4	3:13–19	6: 12–16
Sending out the Twelve	10: 5–15	6: 7–13	9: 1–6
The perils they would face	10: 16–25	13: 9–13	21: 12–17
Fears and faith	10: 26–33		12: 2–7
Sword and sacrifice	10: 34–39		12: 51–53
Welcome and water	10: 40–42	9: 41	
Questions from prison	11: 1–19		7: 18–35
Criticism of certain towns	11: 20–24		10: 13–15
Revelation and invitation	11: 25–30		10: 21–22
The cornfield controversy	12: 1–8	2: 23–28	6: 1–5
The synagogue 'scandal'	12: 9–14	3: 1–6	6: 6–11
God's chosen servant	12: 15–21		
The Beelzebul argument	12: 22–32	3: 20–30	11: 14–23
A tree and its fruit	12: 33–37		6: 43–45
The demand for a 'sign'	12: 38–42	8: 11–12	11: 29–32
The parable of the spirits	12: 43–45		11: 24–26
Jesus's family	12: 46–50	3: 31–35	8: 19–21
The sower and the soil	13: 1–9	4: 1–9	8: 4–8
The purpose of parables	13: 10–17	4: 10–12	8: 9–10
The sower parable explained	13: 18–23	4: 13–20	8: 11–15
The weeds in the wheat	13: 24–30		
The smallest seed	13: 31–32	4: 30–32	13: 18–19
The yeast in the bread	13: 33		13: 20–21
The use of parables	13: 34–35	4: 33–34	
The weeds parable explained	13: 36–43		
Hidden treasures	13: 44–46		
The parable of the fishing-net	13: 47–50		
New truths discovered	13: 51–52		
The 'set-back' at Nazareth	13: 53–58	6: 1–6	(4: 16–30 similar)
Death of John the Baptist	14: 1–12	6: 14–29	9: 7–9
Feeding the five thousand	14: 13–21 (also in John 6: 1–15)	6: 30–44	9: 10–17
Walking on the water	14: 22–32 (also in John 6: 16–21)	6: 45–52	
Healing by the lake	14: 34–36	6: 53–56	

116

Incident	Matthew	Mark	Luke
The teaching traditions	15: 1–9	7: 1–13	
What really defiles a person	15: 10–20	7: 14–23	
A foreigner's faith	15: 21–28	7: 24–30	
More healing by the lake	15: 29–31		
Feeding the four thousand	15: 32–39	8: 1–10	
Signs of the times	16: 1–4	8: 11–13	12: 54–56
The 'leaven' of the Pharisees	16: 5–12	8: 14–21	
Peter's 'confession'	16: 13–20	8: 27–30	9: 18–21
The first prediction of death	16: 21–28	8: 31–9: 1	9: 22–27
The transfiguration	17: 1–13	9: 2–13	9: 28–36
The epileptic boy	17: 14–21	9: 14–29	9: 37–43
The second prediction of death	17: 22–23	9: 30–32	9: 44–45
Paying the temple tax	17: 24–27		
The example of a child	18: 1–5	9: 33–37	9: 46–48
Causing a child to stumble	18: 6–9	9: 42–48	17: 1–2
Parable of the lost sheep	18: 10–14		15: 3–7
The attitude towards offenders	18: 15–20		
The parable of the two debtors	18: 21–35		
Marriage and divorce	19: 1–12	10: 1–12	
Blessing the children	19: 13–15	10: 13–16	18: 15–17
The would-be disciple	19: 16–22	10: 17–22	18: 18–23
The danger of riches	19: 23–30	10: 23–31	18: 24–30
The dissatisfied workers	20: 1–16		
The third prediction of death	20: 17–19	10: 32–34	18: 31–34
A mother's request	20: 20–28	10: 35–45	
Healing the blind at Jericho	20: 29–34	10: 46–52	18: 35–43
Riding into Jerusalem	21: 1–11 (also in John 12: 12–19)	11: 1–11	19: 28–40
Cleansing the temple	21: 12–17 (also in John 2: 13–22)	11: 15–19	19: 45–48
The fig-tree 'mystery'	21: 18–22	11: 12–14	
By whose authority?	21: 23–27	11: 27–33	20: 1–8
The parable of the two brothers	21: 28–32		
The parable of the vineyard	21: 33–46	12: 1–12	20: 9–19
The parable of the wedding feast	22: 1–14		(14: 16–24 similar)
The question of taxes to Caesar	22: 15–22	12: 13–17	20: 20–26
Whose wife will she be?	22: 23–33	12: 18–27	20: 27–40
The greatest commandment	22: 34–40	12: 28–34	10: 25–28
Comparison with David	22: 41–46	12: 35–37	20: 41–44
Criticism of the pride and pretence of the religious leaders	23: 1–12	12: 38–39	20: 45–47
The seven 'woes'	23: 13–36	12: 38–40	11: 42–54
Jerusalem's refusal to accept Jesus	23: 37–39		13: 34–35
The coming destruction of the temple	24: 1–2	13: 1–2	21: 5–6
Impending sorrows and persecutions	24: 3–28	13: 3–23	21: 7–24
The coming of the Son of Man	24: 29–31	13: 24–27	21: 25–28

Incident	Matthew	Mark	Luke
Lessons from the fig tree	24: 32–35	13: 28–31	21: 29–33
Be on the alert!	24: 36–44	13: 32–37	17: 26–30
The conscientious servant	24: 45–51		12: 41–48
The ten bridesmaids	25: 1–13		
The three servants	25: 14–30		(19: 11–27
The sheep and the goats	25: 31–46		similar)
The plot to kill Jesus	26: 1–5	14: 1–2	22: 1–2
The annointing at Bethany	26: 6–13	14: 3–9	
	(John 12: 1–8 similar)		
Judas agrees to betray Jesus	26: 14–16	14: 10–11	22: 3–6
Preparations for the Last Supper	26: 17–19	14: 12–16	22: 7–13
The Last Supper	26: 20–29	14: 17–25	22: 19–30
	(see also 1 Corinthians 11: 23–26)		
Peter's denial predicted	26: 30–35	14: 27–31	22: 31–34
The prayers in Gethsemane	26: 36–46	14: 32–42	22: 39–46
The arrest	26: 47–56	14: 43–50	22: 47–53
The Jewish trial	26: 57–68	14: 53–65	22: 63–71
Peter's denial of Jesus	26: 69–75	14: 66–72	22: 54–62
Jesus is taken to Pilate	27: 1–2	15: 1	23: 1–2
Judas's suicide	27: 3–10		
	(see also Acts 1: 18–19)		
The Roman trial	27: 11–26	15: 2–15	23: 1–25
The jeering at Jesus	27: 27–31	15: 16–20	
The crucifixion	27: 32–44	15: 21–32	23: 26–43
The death of Jesus	27: 45–56	15: 33–41	23: 44–49
The burial	27: 57–61	15: 42–47	23: 50–56
The guard put on the tomb	27: 62–66		
The Resurrection	28: 1–10	16: 1–10	24: 1–12
Bribery of the soldiers	28: 11–15		
Appearance and commission to the Eleven in Galilee	28: 16–20		